BUSINESS LITERACY

SURVIVAL GUIDE

for

HR PROFESSIONALS

BUSINESS LITERACY
SURVIVAL GUIDE
for
HR PROFESSIONALS

Dr. Regan W. Garey, CPA

Society for Human Resource Management
Alexandria, Virginia
www.shrm.org

Strategic Human Resource Management India
Mumbai, India
www.shrmindia.org

Society for Human Resource Management
Haidian District Beijing, China
www.shrm.org/cn

Dedications

To my editor and mother, Doris Whalen, for her continuous support and excellent editing, my loving husband, Frank, and children, Meggan and Gerry, of whom I am very proud. For my deceased father who, I know in my heart, sees this milestone in my life.

Acknowledgements

To my friend and colleague, Dr. Pat Buhler, without whom I may not have written this book and for my publisher, Christopher Anzalone, for his support.

The Society for Human Resource Management (SHRM) is the world's largest association devoted to human resource management. Representing more than 250,000 members in over 140 countries, the Society serves the needs of HR professionals and advances the interests of the HR profession. Founded in 1948, SHRM has more than 575 affiliated chapters within the United States and subsidiary offices in China and India. Visit SHRM Online at www.shrm.org.

Interior and Cover Design: Shirley E.M. Raybuck

Library of Congress Cataloging-in-Publication Data

Garey, Regan W., 1959-
Business literacy survival guide for HR professionals / Regan Garey. -- 1st ed.
p. cm.
Includes bibliographical references and index.
ISBN 978-1-58644-205-7
1. Personnel management. 2. Strategic planning. 3. Accounting. I. Title.
HF5549.G3176 2011
658.15--dc22
2010039097

10-0459

Contents

Preface

Individuals who chose to become HR professionals frequently made that decision to help people attain their career goals. The HR professional is often seen as the liaison between the organization's management and the employees. Most HR professionals would rather work with people instead of numbers.

As organizations have become increasingly more complex via global expansion and mergers and acquisitions, and as the sophistication level and knowledge base of employees has exploded, the HR community has often not kept pace.

Being a Business Leader

For the HR professional, there are numerous benefits to becoming a more credible, business-savvy employee. First, knowing more allows for more opportunities to move up instead of out of the organization. Second, when the HR professional can learn and internalize core competencies (see chapter 2 for details), he or she can make a more visible, true contribution to his or her organization. Third, with knowledge comes power. I believe this statement 100 percent. When an individual can obtain more knowledge, he or she can be more confident and more assertive within the organizational setting because there is the belief that his or her opinion matters and is based on facts.

Ignorance of the Business Is *Not* an Option

Years ago, HR professionals were often satisfied to just do their jobs. They knew all the many facets of their positions and were not that interested in being a strategic partner with other management in the organization. This is no longer the case. HR professionals are becoming increasingly aware that they must be more visible, viable members of the team. They also want to enhance their reputations as competent, well-rounded, knowledgeable employees and members of management.

The author of the well-known article "Why We Hate HR" lists the many perceptions of the HR community, many of which are negative.[1] These perceptions, which are held by many organizations' employees and management, must be not only acknowledged but also challenged. This is an opportunity for change. This article blatantly states that the HR community has alienated itself from other organizational departments and the lack of business acumen has put a nail in the HR community's collective coffin.

This startling reminder that the HR profession is viewed negatively by many organizations' management and employees is the impetus for this book. *Business Literacy Survival Guide for HR Professionals* will help bridge the gap between human resources and other levels of management, thereby leveling the playing field.

How can this be accomplished?

When HR professionals can speak the language of business (i.e., accounting), their peers and superiors within the organization will include them in the organizational decision-making process.

This book will explain business literacy terms and concepts via numerous examples that are applicable to the HR role. The book will not attempt to train readers in intermediate or advanced accounting concepts. Instead, HR professionals will be exposed to the multiple financial ramifications of what they do within the organization. Specifically, HR departmental decisions and day-to-day operations will be related to the financial statements and other financial decisions made by management.

While this book won't turn you, as an HR professional, into a financial expert, it will provide enough guidance and insight into the world of business finance to promote a greater awareness and appreciation when helping to manage the company. Specifically, the HR world, by definition, is intimately connected to workforce planning, talent recruitment, training and development, performance management, salary and benefit design and administration, knowledge management, succession planning, etc. *These core HR functions are all intertwined with and codependent upon the financial health of the organization.* Ultimately, an enhanced and more concrete understanding of business finance will make you, as an HR professional, more successful in your career and will make you a greater asset to your organization (pun intended!).

In 2009, a business literacy survey was distributed electronically to a Society for Human Resource Management statewide membership. Approximately 100 SHRM members in this mid-Atlantic area of the United States participated in this short survey and the results are referred to throughout this book. See Appendix A to view the results.

CHAPTER 1

Human Resources as Strategic Partner

What is strategy? Strategic thinking and strategic management involve viewing the "big picture" of the organization and devising ways to get all levels of management to buy into the strategies. Historically, human resources was rarely considered to be part of the team of strategic managers, but that is beginning to change. For this change to continue, human resources must understand some basic tenets of strategic management.

Strategic management involves three basic assumptions:

- Companies and the competitive environment in which they operate are dynamic in nature
- The formulation of strategy and its implementation must be completely connected
- Strategic leaders must take an active role in implementing their strategies

Human resources is often not consulted when management develops and implements the strategic plan. But rather than waiting for an invitation to contribute, HR professionals today are increasingly asking to be involved because they are more cognizant of their potential role as a partner in this process. To maximize their contributions, HR professionals must understand and become well-versed in each of the following steps. First, analyze the vision and mission of the organization and ingrain them into the HR consciousness. Next, study the organization's specific goals and objectives. Third, recognize that the strategy is developed based on the organization's goals and objectives. Last and perhaps most important, ensure that the strategy is implemented effectively and efficiently.

Strategy Is Active and Multi-Dimensional

For human resources to be an active partner in the organization's strategic planning, there must be sufficient knowledge about the multiple aspects of strategy and financial concepts. As seen below, many aspects of strategy are financially based. According to Mason Carpenter and William Gerard Sanders, there are five dimensions of the business strategy diamond.[1]

The first dimension and fundamental basis for strategic planning is economic logic. Economic logic is the overall core for strategy or decision-making at the organizational top level. It involves characteristics such as lowest costs through advantages, premium prices due to unmatchable service, etc.

On the perimeter of the strategic-level diamond are the remaining four dimensions:

- *Arenas.* Where is our focus? What product categories? Which value-creation strategies? Which market segments?
- *Vehicles.* How will we get there? Internal development? Joint ventures? Alliances?
- *Differentiators.* How will we win? Image? Customization? Price? Speed to market?
- *Staging and pricing.* What is our speed and sequence of moves? Speed of expansion? Sequence of initiatives?

Vision, Mission, and Strategy

Successful organizations align their vision, mission, and strategy. To ensure that this occurs, an organization should first ensure that its vision and mission wherein the organization's values and fundamental purpose for existence are developed. Next, the organization should incorporate its strategic goals and objectives, which must be specific in nature and have measurable outcomes. Measurable outcomes often means quantitative instead of qualitative analysis. This book will help human resources understand some of these critical metrics, i.e., what they are and why they matter. These metrics will include numerous items such as financial ratios and other quantifiable measures. Last, the strategy itself is developed and implemented. Again, ideally, there is an organization-wide assimilation of this strategy and it is not solely imposed from top management.

Business Strategies

Michael Porter is a well-known strategic management researcher and writer. His theories of generic strategic positions are well-accepted in both the academic world and by businesses. He developed the following options:

- low-cost leadership;
- differentiation;
- focused cost leadership; and
- focused differentiation.[2]

Human resources must be acutely aware of the organization's positioning since this choice drives many financial decisions within the organization.

Low-Cost Advantage Financial Concepts

The costs associated with this strategic focus will be discussed later in the book but are worthy of mention here. They include fixed costs, variable costs, marginal costs, average costs, and economies of scale.

Differentiation

Often a company's products or services are accepted if its customers are willing to pay a premium for certain product or service features. This willingness to pay a higher price means the company must sustain a financial gap between the price and the costs of producing the product or service.

Regardless of the positioning chosen (i.e., low-cost leadership, differentiation, focused cost leadership, or focused differentiation), each company will fall into one of three categories regarding its relationships with its competitors. The company will either be a first mover, second mover, or fast follower. When an organization is a first mover, the organization undertakes more risks than its competition since it is the first organization to aggressively carve out market share for itself. If the organization is a second mover, then the opportunities for excessive profits are lower compared to the first mover but there are fewer risks involved in going into that particular market. Fast followers make up the majority of companies; they recognize the economic opportunities in quickly entering that particular market, and they carve out a segment of the market for themselves after the product or service has a proven level of demand from consumers. Again, this strategic decision will ultimately have financial ramifications.

Return on *Your* Investment

As an HR professional, what can you expect to gain from reading, understanding, and incorporating these business literacy concepts into your career? What would be your expected return on this investment?

- Respect from peers and decision-makers within your organization
- Enhanced promotion opportunities
- Understanding of the future financial stability of your organization
- Knowing the growth potential for your organization relative to its competitors
- Better decision making skills
- Stronger understanding and appreciation of strategic decisions made by top management
- Understanding of cash management
- Knowledge of where fraud, waste, and abuse can be minimized

• Insights of what upcoming major legislative changes may impact your organization

The Importance of HR Leadership Qualities

For any individual within an organization, leadership qualities and characteristics can open doors to management positions. Credibility, intelligence, interpersonal skills, emotional intelligence, and a myriad of other leadership qualities help an individual move up the corporate ladder. In some cases, individuals with these enviable qualities decide to launch their own businesses and become entrepreneurs.

Leaders must possess multiple qualities. Emotional intelligence is an area that is somewhat interpretative so studying emotional intelligence attributes has been popular for many years. This author has done substantial research on emotional intelligence, for example, and maintains that the most successful people are ones who are emotionally intelligent. Leaders who are emotionally intelligent know themselves well and can understand others.

Another well-accepted leadership quality comes from Linda Martin and David Mutchler in *Fail-Safe Leadership*, where they describe the SMART system of goal achievement.[3] They maintain that goals must

• be **S**pecific,

• be **M**easurable,

• be **A**ttainable,

• be **R**ealistic, and

• have a specific **T**arget date.

This SMART system can arguably be one way that human resources can view their intricate role within the organization and how they can be a part of management solutions.

For example, if you, as an HR professional, have the goal of being more of a key player in management and strategic decision making, then analyze your goals with this SMART system. One of your goals could easily be that you need to be more financially literate or financially intelligent. That is a specific goal. It is measurable, if you read this book and quiz yourself on what you learned. There is no doubt that this goal is attainable but also just beyond the natural reach of many HR professionals. This goal is realistic if you relate as many concepts as possible in this book to your career. Try to assimilate the information and read over the concepts enough times that the information becomes very familiar to you. The target date could be one month or three months from now as an example.

In any case, as you read this book keep in mind that this newly obtained business literacy knowledge must not be kept to yourself. Instead, as you read about these many financial concepts, consider how you can use them now and in the future as you fine-tune your leadership capabilities.

CHAPTER 2

The Seven Competencies

In recent years there has been a renewed enthusiasm within the HR profession. Open-minded, visionary members of the HR community are developing and promoting their profession. Several authors' and researchers' findings have gained so much popular support that they have changed the paradigm in the HR community.

What is all the excitement about?

HR competencies are in the forefront of numerous discussions, conferences, and Society for Human Resource Management (SHRM) meetings. For example, in the well-received book, *HR Competencies: Mastery at the Intersection of People and Business*,[1] the authors illustrate the evolved "HR Competency Model" (see figure 2.1). In this chapter we will explore the application of these HR competencies to financial concepts.

Figure 2.1

Core HR Competencies

We start with discussion of the widely accepted six HR competencies (see figure 2.2), add our business literacy competency, and build from there.

Figure 2.2

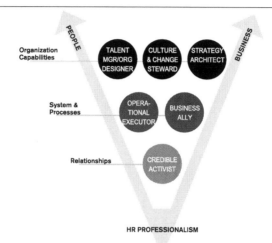

Your goal is to read and understand the key financial concepts related to your career and organization. That is where this survival guide will come in handy over and over again. Use this book as a resource throughout your career. Refer to it before management meetings or before you deal with your peers, subordinates, suppliers, or customers. Show them you can "talk the talk" and know the language of business: accounting.

Credible Activist

This key competency is the cornerstone of the other competencies, according to Dave Ulrich. Basically, without this first competency the other competencies are less meaningful. It can be summed up as being accountable, taking initiative, and doing the right things the right way.

The Credible Activist focuses primarily on relationships and relationship building.

Cultural and Change Steward

Human resources has always been an integral part of promoting corporate culture. Since passage of the Sarbanes-Oxley Act of 2002 (SOX),[2] the focus on ethical cultures has become even more important. According to Ulrich, of all the competencies, Cultural Steward is the second highest predictor of performance of human resources on both an individual and departmental level. In addition, change management is a key aspect of human resources.

Talent Manager/Organizational Designer

Talent management focuses on how employees get hired, get promoted, and make lateral moves, as well as how employees move out of the organization. Ulrich believes that human resources focuses too much on talent acquisition instead of organizational design. Ultimately, the talent of the employees must be aligned with the organizational structure.

Strategy Architect

This competency involves being able to recognize business trends and their impact on the business, while also identifying potential roadblocks and opportunities. This may be described as a SWOT (strengths, weaknesses, opportunities, and threats) analysis.

Business Ally

Human resources can and should be actively involved in the business decision making within the organization by understanding how the business makes money, who the customers are, and why customers buy the company's products or services. Having business intelligence is a critical steppingstone to having a "seat at the table."

Operational Executor

Some may argue that transactional duties such as drafting, adapting and implementing policies are the drudgery aspect of human resources. But Ulrich argues that these nuts-and-bolts activities are also critical to the financial success of the organization.

Business Literacy

Financially literate individuals understand the interconnectedness of business decisions. They know how to interpret the financial statements; financial ratios; internal controls; red flags for financial waste, fraud, and abuse; and the new legislative acts that can have a tremendous impact on the accounting framework of their organization.

Credible Activist Aligned with Business Literacy

Integrity, self-confidence, and knowledge. Harnessing these strengths simultaneously can lead to tremendous potential for an HR professional to become a strong voice within his or her organization. The Credible Activist must capitalize on both interpersonal and technical skills since these are the two cornerstones of this competency.

Per Ulrich's research, the four characteristics of Credible Activist include:

- Delivering results with integrity
- Sharing information
- Building relationships of trust
- A certain level of assertiveness

One of the fastest ways anyone can lose credibility is to be a loud voice in the organization without knowledge of the business *or* to be a wallflower with immense technical and business knowledge but no voice.

This author proposes that there is a correlation between the characteristics of the Credible Activist and having business acumen. Specifically, understanding the concepts and terminology of business will allow the HR professional more opportunities to share accurate information with colleagues within the organization.

Relationships that are built on trust include the essentials of honesty and open communication. The Credible Activist understands the goals of the organization and can communicate those goals in an effective, professional manner.

People at *all* levels of an organization usually have know-how that can be of use to decision makers. Human resources should ask to what extent information is widely shared in their organization so that those who make decisions have access to such knowledge.

Alignment Between Business Intelligence and the Credible Activist

In this hypothetical example, the HR manager, Meggan Logan, approached Gerry Smith, the CEO of the organization, with a request for new computers for the HR department. Knowing that the CEO could be skeptical of this request, Meggan took it upon herself to first research the viability of this request. She did a cost-benefit analysis in which she was able to document that the new computers would increase productivity and reduce overtime pay within her department.

She reviewed the cash flow statement and understood that the timing of her request was important and that she had to understand the cash sources and uses throughout the year. She also knew *not* to rely that much on the income statement, which showed that the organization had earned a positive net income, since she knew that income and cash are not necessarily the same thing (more on that later). By being an informed member of the management team, Meggan made a financially sound request based on her knowledge of the financial situation of the organization.

Her request was granted by the CEO, who now viewed her as a manager who was looking out for her subordinates within her department but was also aware of the financial constraints of the organization. The level of trust between the HR manager and her department and between the CEO and the HR manager was enhanced because the information communicated by the HR manager was based on financially sound facts.

Cultural and Change Steward Alignment with Business Intelligence

Ethics and accounting and finance are strongly interwoven. If the HR department is not a strong advocate and promoter of an ethical corporate culture, a feeling of laissez faire (do as you want to) can permeate the entire organization.

As will be discussed in chapter 10, instituting and continually communicating to all employees about the whistle-blower option is the responsibility of human resources. This author maintains that the whistle-blower provision of the SOX is a back-up mechanism for organization-wide promotion of an ethical culture. Some smaller or non-publicly traded companies have not been required to institute an anonymous whistle-blower provision as part of the passage of SOX. However, many organizations have set up some sort of procedure in which employees can anonymously report unethical or fraudulent activities.

Human resources needs to be keenly aware that the culture drives the way employees view their role within the organization. For example, if there is a careless way of analyzing revenue recognition and the accounting department is not continually vigilant in its recording of revenue only when it is actually earned, other employees may sense that "anything goes" in that organization.

Unethical or erroneous transactions are often recorded and go undetected until they end up in the financial statements or until the auditors conduct their annual audit. Having management rather than auditors find errors or fraud is paramount to the viability of the organization, the sense of employee accountability, and investors' perceptions of the organization.

Think about Enron and the role that human resources could have played if they were more aware of what can go wrong in an organization's financial reporting procedures and techniques. The ensuing implosion of Enron speaks volumes about the disaster that can occur when corporate culture is not implicitly and explicitly ethical. The HR professional plays a pivotal role in promoting an ethical culture.

One way to verify that key management practices such as budgeting are accurately aligned with the culture is to conduct a culture audit. This author has created a corporate culture audit for this scenario. See the textbox for a small sampling of the questions.

Corporate Culture Audit—Sample Questions

1. Corporate culture may be defined as management style, commitment to deliver quality products and services, belief in staff training and development, and encouragement of open communication. Open corporate cultures can be characterized as having management who encourage the free flow of information within the organization. In general, how important is it in this organization that management encourages high-quality, frequent communication with employees?

   Answer:
   ☐ Very Important ☐ Important ☐ Somewhat important

2. Open communication in an organization means that employees are encouraged to discuss with management all issues related to their job responsibilities even if the issue is of a sensitive nature. To what degree would you characterize the culture within this organization as having a well-developed system of open communication?

   Answer:
   ☐ Very Open ☐ Open ☐ Somewhat Open ☐ Never Open

Change Steward

The other aspect of this HR competency is change steward. It would be difficult to find any organization, large or small, that is not continually instituting some sort of change. Human resources must be diligent in supporting and promoting change that is occurring. The change can be something as small as a new target market for the organization to something as widespread and monumental as an acquisition or a merger.

Interconnection Between Business Intelligence and Cultural and Change Steward

Software changes are often made within organizations that are undergoing expansion or are seeking cost savings and higher employee productivity. Many archaic forms of organizations still operate with the silo system wherein departments are making decisions independently of each other. Software changes are often instituted in order to integrate procedures and processes across the organization. Software engineers are often deployed to set up processes that input financial information with specific criteria for report format and content.

Human resources can become a key player during and after this process if and when they understand the financial metrics of the organization. For example, during meetings when these changes are being discussed human resources can ask questions of how the information will now be disseminated across departments and functions. Human resources can also recognize which information should come from each aspect of the business and how the end results should appear on the financials.

In this hypothetical example, our HR manager Meggan, along with other top management in the organization, developed an initiative to coordinate the many departments within the organization for improved integration of procedures and policies. Meggan realized that employee productivity could be enhanced with improved communications between the functional areas of the organization. Without integrated systems, Meggan knew that some procedures would continually result in duplicated efforts between various departments and those duplications are costly to the organization. Because Meggan was aware of many financial metrics used to measure employee productivity and profitability in her organization, she was an instrumental part of aligning the HR function with the business aspect of the organization.

Talent Manager/Organizational Designer Aligned with Business Literacy

Historically, human resources has been responsible for recruiting and training the best employees for their organizations. But the story cannot end there anymore. When human resources can assimilate top management's strategic plans into their day-to-day activities (or better yet, be part of them), they can envision how the employees will add value to the organization both now and in the future.

In this hypothetical example, our HR manager, Meggan, had several meetings with the organization's CEO, Gerry Smith, about the immediate need to hire a high-level marketing director. Meggan had anticipated the challenge of deciding on the compensation package that would be offered to the best candidate for the position since she remembered the financial aspect of this decision. During their meetings, Meggan and Gerry looked at the financial statements from the past two years and discussed the benefits costs for the new manager. Issues such as the organization's recent income levels and cash flow were part of their discussions. Since their organization was in the manufacturing business, the issue of the increased overhead costs associated with this new hire had to be discussed. Meggan's business literacy enhanced her strategic decision making role in the organization.

Interconnection Between Business Intelligence and Talent Manager/Organizational Designer

In a recent *Time* magazine article, the founder of Starbucks was featured as he discussed the company's plans to reorganize and change its strategic focus in response to the weak economy.[3] Creating and promoting new products is the focus of the company, which has been struggling to rebound from store closings and lower levels of sales. The other opportunity for the company is more expansion into overseas markets.

How can human resources be involved with this new mindset and strategy? Human resources can propose some new programs to strengthen ties to customers and grocery store owners. Human resources can become directly involved in finding the best people to conduct viability studies for overseas markets. By understanding the potential customers' buying habits and deploying the right salespeople for these newly established regions, human resources can position itself as part of the value chain.

Human resources also plays a key role in the following areas: global workforce assessment, forecasting, recruitment, planning, and development.

Strategy Architect Aligned with Business Literacy

For many years human resources has been a tactical rather than a strategic partner in most organizations. Strategic decisions are made, and human resources is tasked with the tactical or "make things happen" part of the process. When that aspect is the only part human resources sees, it is easy to lose sight of the vision or mission of the organization—especially during times of change.

Opportunity costs exist for every business decision made. Simply stated, if one course of action is undertaken, others cannot be taken simultaneously. It is one key mechanism or mindset to help an organization realize that there are always financial and time constraints and not all opportunities can materialize at the same time.

There are costs and benefits associated with every decision made. The goal is to maximize benefits and minimize costs. But what are those specific costs? If human resources is aware of the numerous costs involved in any decision or project, they are more likely to become part of the solution rather than be an afterthought for top management. For example, understanding fixed overhead costs and variable costs may help human resources be a partner in the decision making process.

Most importantly, if HR professionals understand the financial constraints and opportunities for new strategic directions, there will be more synergies between management of all departments within the organization. Human resources will be on the inside of these key management decision-making processes.

In this hypothetical example, CEO Gerry Smith had asked to meet with all of his top management. Along with other members of management, the HR director, Meggan, was invited to offer her input into the decision of how a potential merger would have an enormous impact on the organization. Trend analysis was one of the many financial tools used during these meetings (more on this topic later). Management assessed the profitability trends and analyzed cost savings that could occur from a merger with another organization. From a strategic architect perspective, Meggan understood the many financial ramifications of this key decision. For example, she realized the importance of reviewing the statement of cash flows to see the sources and uses of cash in recent years, the level of retained earnings to see how much of recent earnings were retained in the organization, etc. Meggan's understanding of the financial strength of her organization gave her more credibility.

Business Ally Aligned with Business Literacy

This competency is the foundation for this book, so it will be approached and discussed in a slightly different manner. Becoming business literate is the most critical aspect of being a member of the decision making team of any organization. A comprehensive understanding of how the organization makes money, expands its market reach, and is financially sound all work in concert to help human resources ask *and* answer financially based questions in a convincing fashion.

Operational Executor Aligned with Business Literacy

In previous decades, HR professionals spent most of their time and energy on this competency. Operational Executor involves systems and processes that human resources both develops and follows up on. Recently there has been an increasing reliance on software systems throughout the organization. All employees including HR professionals have been coaxed or trained into using systems that exist to increase employee productivity and dissemination of information.

Internal controls are the veritable nuts-and-bolts of financial risk management, and they ensure that the financials will truly reflect the organization's business transactions. Internal controls are numerous and varied, but basically they help prevent fraud, waste, and abuse of resources (more on this in chapter 10). Every aspect of the organization must be built on certain processes and procedures. Without these processes and procedures, the organization can tend toward eventual chaos.

Human resources must trust in their organizational structure despite the seemingly overreliance upon rules. Each department must ensure that there are common goals and objectives that are reflected in the processes and procedures. Employees rely on human resources to communicate the organizational goals and objectives.

In this hypothetical example, our HR manager, Meggan, hired a new HR vice president. This new vice president, Larry Lee, had no formal training on the financial aspects of the business but he was a very experienced HR professional. Larry did not recognize the critical aspect of internal controls' role in preventing fraud, waste, and abuse and he had not learned about the financial risks of the business. Larry possessed great interpersonal skills but he lacked the ability to think strategically and he was not aware that the business' departments could evolve into silos. Lack of coordination and communication between functional areas or departments within an organization can lead to an atmosphere of laissez-faire instead of a coordinated effort within the entire organization to reach organizational goals. His lack of business acumen was detrimental to his department and the organization as a whole.

In extreme cases, lack of continuity of processes and procedures throughout the organization will result in cases such as Enron. Enron's accounting scandal could be partially attributable to the corporate culture and lack of strict internal controls. Turning a blind eye to other employees circumventing rules ended up hurting the entire organization. We all know the rest of the story of this financial disaster.

Conclusion

As seen from the numerous examples above, HR competencies from Ulrich's research have so many interconnections to business literacy. As the HR community becomes more knowledgeable about the many financial ramifications of strategic and tactical decisions made within their organizations, they can help their organizations reach their goals and objectives more expeditiously.

CHAPTER 3

The "Big Picture": The Financials

The primary accounting and finance concepts discussed in this book will be ones that directly or indirectly relate to human resources. Before exploring some of those financial concepts, we will pause for a moment to explain some general concepts about how and why businesses operate.

According to a leading financial accounting textbook, "Business activities—planning, financing, investing, and operating—are synthesized into a cohesive picture of how businesses function in a market economy."[1] The quote relates to the "big picture" of the main functions of a for-profit business. This relates to the HR function because human resources is involved with assessment, forecasting, recruitment, planning, and development, as mentioned in chapter 2. Human resources' role is important because without the right people in the right positions, the business will not be able to function efficiently or effectively.

The first stage for any company is formulating a business plan. Next, the company would have to pursue investors and creditors to finance their land, buildings, equipment, labor, etc. These investments are then used to produce goods or services, which are the operating activities of the business.

The following section will define the players in an organization and their primary duties and responsibilities. The players include the following: management, the board of directors, and accounting and finance staff.

Management vs. Owners: Agency Theory

Agency theory should be mentioned at this point as a way to explain individuals' roles within an organization. Agency theory has to do with one individual acting on behalf of another individual. In agency theory, the principal (the one with power) asks an agent to act on his or her behalf. For the purposes of our discussion, management is the agent, and the principal (the party that entrusts the agent to act in their best interests) represents the collective interests of shareholders.

Prior to the Industrial Revolution, American businesses were operated and managed by their owners without the assistance of outside management. As our economy evolved and business owners resembled investors more than workers within businesses, the role of management grew at a tremendous rate.

Much research has been done questioning the true loyalties of management. Is management acting on their own behalf or in the best interests of shareholders?

Ideally, management of all ranks and functional areas of an organization will put the needs of the organization above their own individual needs. However, human resources should be aware that, according to agency theory, there is an implicit struggle between doing what is best for oneself and what is best for the organization. This struggle can become apparent, for example, with management in operations or top management when financial results affect the payment of their management bonuses.

Board of Directors

Many organizations have a board of directors (some nonprofits call it a board of trustees) who are tasked with making strategic-level decisions. Management often presents proposed changes to the board for approval and is supposed to defer to the board if and when there is a difference of opinion. The board has a fiduciary duty to act and make decisions in the best interest of the organization it represents. Board members may be compensated for their time or may work with the organization for no compensation. The latter is often the case with small organizations and/ or nonprofits.

Accountant vs. Financial Manager

Accountants often specialize in different aspects of business. For example, accountants can specialize in tax, audit, financial reporting, governmental accounting, or cost accounting.

Accountants who specialize in tax typically become proficient in either individual tax or corporate tax. Accountants who become auditors can either be independent auditors who visit companies annually to verify the financial reports or become internal auditors who are employees of the organization. Accountants specializing in financial reporting focus on creating and interpreting the financial statements that are discussed in this book. The various levels of government (i.e., federal, state, and local governments) also employ accountants who have specialized knowledge about specifics in government accounting. Cost accountants focus primarily on manufacturing costs or services in which there are numerous types of costs. We will be discussing some aspects of cost accounting when we talk about activity based accounting.

Finance is similar to accounting, and there are many overlapping areas between the two functions. The finance manager's goal is to maximize shareholder wealth. The primary functions of the financial manager (assuming the organization is large enough and complex enough to warrant differentiating between the accounting and finance functions) include:

- *Daily:* credit management, receipt and disbursements of funds, inventory control
- *Occasional:* issuance of stocks and bonds, capital budgeting, and dividend decisions

The Goal of Financial Accounting

The end result or goal of financial accounting is the creation of the financial statements. The financial statements consist of the income statement, the statement of owners' equity, the balance sheet, and the statement of cash flows.

Financial statements are made up of accounts. These are the six categories of accounts:

1. *Assets* are things owned by the business. Examples: cash, accounts receivable (defined below), supplies, equipment, land and buildings.

2. *Liabilities* are what is owed by the business and to be paid to others, such as other companies or the bank (if a loan). Examples: accounts payable (defined below), notes payable (if a loan).

3. *Capital* is what is invested or owned by the shareholders or owner of the business. Equity and capital are used interchangeably.

4. *Revenue* is the sales generated from either a service or sale of a product.

5. *Expenses* are the costs of doing business. Examples: rent expense, commissions paid, and salaries expense.

6. *Withdrawals* are monies taken out of the business if the business is a sole proprietorship (one owner) as compared to *dividends*, which are monies distributed to shareholders if the business is a corporation.

Figure 3.1 illustrates the steps that an accountant would take to ultimately create the financial statements.

Figure 3.1

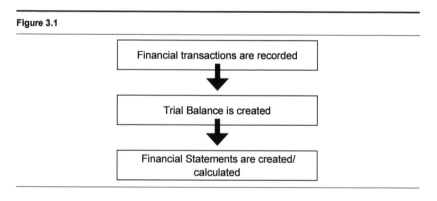

Financial Transactions

After describing the beginning stage of accounting, which is the recording of the financial transactions, we then proceed to discussing and then analyzing the financial statements. Some transactions involve cash, but many do not. The transactions involving cash are often the most visible to many individuals within an organization, but there are many, many other transactions that are recorded by accountants. Several examples follow.

Financial transactions are the nuts-and-bolts of what happens in a business. Some examples include when a business sells its inventory for a profit, when a business purchases supplies, when employees are paid, etc. For every transaction, at least two accounts (recall what the accounts are: assets, liabilities, revenue, expenses, capital, and withdrawals/dividends) are affected. What this means is that two or more accounts change. Hence, the name "double entry accounting."

Here are some examples of financial transactions, starting with the most basic ones first:

1. ABC Company purchases some equipment and pays $12,000. The two accounts affected are cash and equipment. Both are assets. Cash decreases and equipment increases.

2. Salaries are paid, $10,000. The two accounts are salaries expense and cash.

3. Revenue is earned and paid on account, $100,000. The two accounts are revenue and accounts receivable since the customers are being billed vs. paying immediately with cash or its equivalent.

Organizations vary widely in the types and quantity of financial transactions that occur. For example, a service-oriented organization like a CPA firm will not have "costs of *goods* sold" (COGS) since it provides a service rather than selling a tangible product. Retail organizations have COGS. Human resources may be directly affected by the concept of COGS if they are subcontracted out to other businesses for part of their company's operations. For example, they may subcontract or outsource part of the manufacturing process of their company's operations. The COGS would be the cost of the goods that will eventually be completed for the company that employs the HR professional.

Another type of entity is a nonprofit organization. It may organize its accounts slightly differently and use some different terms. For example, nonprofits would have restricted and unrestricted funds.

Each organization may choose to use any number of sub-categories for accounts. Sub-categories provide more detail and information to management, and that is the ultimate goal of accounting. Providing accurate information about the financial transactions of the business gives management the tools to make good short-term and long-term decisions.

Financial transactions can be numerous and, once they have been recorded in journal entries (debits and credits), they are summarized in the trial balance. Here is an example of a trial balance. We will not focus that extensively on this internal document since it is beyond the scope of this book, but the numbers on the trial balance will be used to create the financial statements. Note that the same numbers used in this trial balance will be used to create the subsequent financial statements.

Trial Balance

	Debits	Credits
Cash	$8,000	
Accounts Receivable	$100,000	
Equipment	$12,000	
Accounts Payable		$55,000
Capital		$22,000
Withdrawals	$2,000	
Revenue		$100,000
COGS	$40,000	
Office Salaries Expense	$10,000	
Rent Expenses	$5,000	
Totals	$177,000	$177,000

How the Financial Statements Are Interrelated

The financial statements must be created and calculated in a specific order. After the financial transactions have been recorded and summarized in the trial balance, the financial statements can be calculated.

First. The income statement is calculated since the bottom line of the income statement, net income or loss then goes on the statement of owners' equity.

Second. The statement of owners' equity is calculated because ending capital then goes on the balance sheet.

Third. The balance sheet is calculated.

Fourth. The statement of cash flows can be done any time after the income statement since the statement of cash flows' first line is net income, which comes from the income statement.

Types of Financial Statements

The first financial statement that is calculated is always the income statement. It represents the operating activities of the company. The income statement contains revenue and expenses only. The bottom line is earnings (also called net income), which represent the *profitability* of the company. The shareholders of a company have a strong interest in earnings since they invested their money (capital) into the business in return for a share of the earnings.

The second financial statement is the statement of owners' equity. This statement is calculated in order to track the amount that the owner(s) have invested into the business.

The third financial statement is the balance sheet. It is a valuable statement that shows the amount of assets, liabilities, and capital (equity) at any moment in time. The assets must equal the total liabilities and capital.

The fourth and most complex financial statement is the statement of cash flows. The first line on this statement is net income, which comes from the income statement. The goal of this financial statement is to explain the many financial items that either decrease or increase cash. (The statement of cash flows will be discussed in more detail in chapter 6.)

Role of Accountants, Auditors, and Management

Accountants create the financial statements, and auditors analyze and verify the financial numbers at year-end. Accountants and managers are mindful of the fact that auditors will scrutinize and question many aspects of the financials. Therefore, accountants are responsible for correctly categorizing the organization's specific expenses, for example, instead of putting many expenses under the category "miscellaneous expenses." Remember, cost of goods sold (COGS) will only exist if the organization is purchasing an item, such as shoes, that will be sold later for a profit. Service-oriented organizations do not have COGS on their income statements.

Mid-level managers are often held accountable for maximizing gross profit, which is the difference between sales and COGS. Human resources should be aware that there are numerous combinations of ways that sales and COGS can cause major changes in gross profit. Here are some ways:

- Increase or decrease in sales volume

- Increase or decrease in sales price

- Increase or decrease in cost per unit (COGS discussed above)

	2011	2010	2009
Net revenue	$45,000	$47,900	$42,687
Cost of sales	$(23,900)	$(24,788)	$(21,004)
Gross profit	$21,100	$23,112	$21,683
Gross profit ratio	46.89%	48.25%	50.80%

Note: Gross profit ratios equals gross profit divided by net revenue.

What's on the Financial Statements?

As a reminder, the six categories of accounts that make up the fundamental components of the financial statements are assets, liabilities, capital, revenue, expenses, and withdrawals/dividends. In the most basic terms, the financial statements contain:

- The income statement: Revenue *minus* Expenses *equals* Net Income

- The statement of owners' equity: Capital *plus* Net Income *minus* Withdrawals *equals* Ending Capital

- The balance sheet: Assets *equals* Liabilities *plus* Ending Capital

- The statement of cash flows starts with net income from the income statement and it ends with ending cash from the balance sheet

Who Uses Financial Statements—And How

The financial statements can be viewed as summaries of much (but not all) of the financial transactions that occur within an organization. Many of the numbers on the financial statements are a compilation of hundreds if not thousands of transactions that occur within and affect the organization.

Who needs to understand the financial statements? Just about everyone! Investors need to know about the balance sheet since it contains information about ending balances in an organization's assets and liabilities. Investors also want to know about the company's income from the income statement, and they may have an interest in the cash flow statement, which explains the change in cash between last year and this year.

Employees and management also need to have a complete understanding of the financial statements for their organization since these statements "tell a story" about the organization's strengths and weaknesses. For example, if the balance sheet shows a small amount of cash, what can that tell management? Perhaps the company's customers are not paying in a timely fashion and too much credit has been extended to customers. It could also be that the cash balance is low because the company does not want to have idle cash not earning interest income and it has chosen to invest the money in long-term or short-term investments.

Informed users of financial statements can see both the opportunities and the challenges facing an organization by reading between the lines of the financials. Some red flags can be seen through analysis of the financials. For example, if the statement of cash flows shows a large increase in accounts receivable between last year and this year, a company may want to ask that customers pay in a more timely fashion or may want to impose penalties for late payment. These are just some of the hundreds of ways that the financial statements (and their associated calculations including ratios as discussed later) can provide unique and valuable insights into the organization.

Revenue Can Be Manipulated

Knowing how and why sales revenue increased or decreased is critical because the story behind the numbers differs depending on what caused the change. For example, if the company's sales increased dramatically from last year to this year, it could be due to a large increase in selling price and/or a large decrease in the original cost of the item to the company. The strategic opportunity for the HR professional is finding out what caused the spike in revenue. Is there a true business reason for the selling price increase, or is the business being too optimistic about its customers' willingness to pay this higher price, thus possibly jeopardizing the company's long-term market share as customers start buying elsewhere?

Human resources plays a direct role in providing more opportunities for companies to generate higher sales levels since human resources is involved in the talent acquisition and development of management, including the hiring, training, and performance assessment of individuals who make effective business decisions. The decisions made by these employees can help grow the company and its sales levels. Financial statements are linked by design. Below you will see the example of the three financial statements that clearly illustrate this.

Now that we have discussed how revenue (i.e., sales) can be manipulated, let's take a look at an example of an income statement:

Bolton Company Income Statement December 31, 2010	
Revenue	$100,000*
Cost of Goods Sold (COGS)	$40,000**
Gross Margin	$60,000 △
General and Administrative Expenses:	
Office Supplies	$10,000 Ψ
Rent Expense	$5,000 Ψ
Net Income	$45,000 †

* Revenue *equals* the number of units *multiplied* by the price.
** COGS is what the company paid for the units.
△ Gross Margin equals Revenue minus COGS.
Ψ Deduct from gross margin.
† This is the bottom line/earnings.

Note that other types of expenses can include supplies expense, recruiting expense, depreciation expense, interest expense, etc. Revenue can be put into several categories, such as by product or type of service. The amount of detail shown in the financial statements is decided on by management, which directs accountants' work.

Remember, management needs to make accurate business decisions based on the information provided on the financials.

Statement of Owners' Equity

Beginning Capital	$22,000*
Net Income	$45,000**
Withdrawals	$2,000 ᐃ
Ending Capital	$65,000 †

* Defined below.
** From the Income Statement above.
ᐃ Defined below. This amount is deducted from the combined total of the beginning capital and the net income.
† See below.

Balance Sheet

	Assets	Capital and Liabilities
Cash	$8,000	
Accounts Payable		$55,000
Accounts Receivable	$100,000*	
Capital		$65,000
Equipment	$12,000	
Totals	$120,000	$120,000

*Defined above.

HR professionals may not be directly involved in creation of the financials, but just knowing how to navigate and use a spreadsheet software package is helpful for those situations if and when other managers ask human resources to make changes to a spreadsheet. (Use a spreadsheet software if you want to make any number-crunching easier. You can change a number or two and your answers recalculate instantly!)

Cost-Benefit Analysis

When analyzing anything in business, keep in mind that managers consider the cost-benefit of that analysis. In other words, is the time investment worthwhile and will the analysis render some benefits in excess of the costs?

Human resources can use cost-benefit analysis in initiatives like diversity or sexual harassment training. Another example related to human resources is whether or not some of the HR functions should be outsourced. So many decisions can be analyzed from this cost-benefit perspective. Costs can include monetary or other resources, such as time and effort expended.

Cash management is so critical to financial survival that we now take a look at two components of cash management for all organizations. All organizations, regardless of their size and scope of operations, must effectively balance accounts receivable (the money owed to the organization by customers) and accounts payable (the money owed by the organization to other companies). We will discuss both accounts receivable and accounts payable next.

Importance of Accounts Receivable and Accounts Payable

As a reminder, accounts receivable is an asset, and it is the amount of money that the company's customers or clients owe the company. Typically, customers or clients pay what they owe the company within 30 or 60 days from when the sale occurred.

On the other hand, accounts payable is a short-term or current liability in which the organization has purchased from other businesses. Examples include supplies purchased on account or the telephone bill due next month.

Net Credit Position

Companies typically attempt to balance their accounts payable (future monies out) with their accounts receivable (future monies in). Having a positive net credit balance is critical to cash management. Net credit balance means taking the accounts receivable and netting or subtracting the accounts payable. Basically, having more money coming in than going out is always better for the financial health of the organization. Having a positive rather than a negative number is best. If more money is going out than is coming in, the organization may have some cash flow challenges and might even have to get a short-term loan to cover its day-to-day operating expenses.

For example, Boorer Company usually takes 20 days to pay for its average daily credit purchases of $12,000. Its average daily sales are $11,000, and it collects accounts in 28 days. We will be calculating its net credit position.

Step One: compute accounts receivable and accounts payable. First, accounts receivable equals the average daily credit sales multiplied by the average *collection* period. In this example, accounts receivable equals $11,000 multiplied by the 28 days, which equals $308,000. Second, accounts payable equals the average daily *credit* purchases multiplied by the average *payment* period. In other words, accounts payable equals $12,000 multiplied by 20 days, which equals $240,000.

Step Two: subtract accounts payable from accounts receivable to find the net credit position. In our example, this means $308,000 minus $240,000 equals $68,000, which is a positive net credit position. By the way, we start with accounts receivable because that would be a positive number or inflow of cash, from which we then subtract the negative number, or accounts payable.

What does this mean? In this case, the company's monies in via accounts receivable exceed its monies out via accounts payable. In other words, more money is coming in than going out. The company has a positive net credit position. This is part of cash management, as discussed above. All companies must balance money in and money out.

Accounts Receivable Aging Report

Accounts receivable is often a large part of the organization's current assets. Recall that accounts receivable represents what customers owe the business for products and/or services purchased. Some customers are diligent about paying the business in a timely manner, and some customers do not pay on time or at all.

Accounts receivable aging reports are important because companies may be extending too much credit to their customers (for example, see table 3.1). This report shows the time between when a payment is due and when it is received. Some customers take advantage of an organization's not charging them interest on unpaid balances. When customers owe the business a disproportionately high dollar amount for too long, there is the high probability that the customers will not pay the organization. Collection agencies sometimes have to be contacted to collect monies owed the organization for many months. This can happen when customers no longer need the organization's services or product.

Table 3.1 Example of an Accounts Receivable Aging Report

CUSTOMER AGING	0-30 Days	31-60 Days	61-90 Days	Over 90 Days
A. Jones	750			
K. Smith	850	250		
L. Whenam			950	
S. Rimal				3,000
R. Kates			1,008	
L. Saar			750	
Total	$1,600	$250	$2,708	$3,000

Sometimes cash-strapped companies choose to sell their accounts receivable to an outside party for a percentage of the total. This is called accounts receivable factoring. Companies can sell their receivables to a company and the outside party will give them, for example, 90 cents on the dollar.

Income Statement

Comprehensive Example of Financial Statements
ABC Corporation
Income Statement For the Year Ended December 31, 2011

Sales	$270,000 *
Cost of goods sold	(120,000) **
Gross profit	$ 150,000
Selling, general, and administrative expenses	(30,000)
Earnings from operations (operating income)	$ 120,000
Interest expense	(3,000)***
Earnings before taxes	$ 117,000
Income tax expense	(10,000)
Net income	$ 107,000****

* Sales = Revenue = Selling price x quantity sold
** Cost of goods sold = the cost of the inventory to the company that will be sold to customers
*** Interest expense = implicitly shows the level of debt that company has incurred
****Net income = the "bottom line"

Statement of Owners' Equity

Paid-in capital:	
Common stock	$10,000 *
Retained earnings:	
Beginning balance	$15,000
Net income for the year	107,000 **
Less: Dividends declared and paid during the year	(7,000)
Ending balance	$115,000
Total owners' equity (capital)	$125,000***

* Common Stock = number of shares of stock sold x price per share
** Net income was calculated above in the Income Statement
***Total owners' equity= capital= amount the owner(s) have invested into the company

Balance Sheet

December 31, 2010

Assets:	
Cash	$ 35,000
Accounts receivable	40,000 *
Inventory	37,000**
Total current assets	$112,000
Equipment	120,000***
Less: Accumulated depreciation	(52,000)
	68,000
Total assets	$180,000
Liabilities:	
Accounts payable	$ 15,000****
Long-term debt	40,000
Total liabilities	$ 55,000
Ending capital	$125,000*****
Total liabilities and capital	$180,000

*Accounts receivable = the amount that customers still owe the business for products and/or services sold to them
** Inventory = what will be ultimately sold to customers. Recorded at original cost not the price to be charged to customers upon its sale.
***Equipment = recorded at original cost regardless of its value today
****Accounts payable = amount the business owes other businesses for services or products purchased
*****Ending Capital = calculated from the Statement of Owners' Equity (above)

Business Ally Competency and Asset and Expense Classifications

There are some common misconceptions that individuals learning accounting often have. There are often situations wherein individuals misinterpret how the transaction will be interpreted and recorded in the company's accounting records.

The following examples touch on the often misinterpreted classification of expenses versus assets. Accountants are responsible for correctly categorizing transactions, often with the assistance of their bookkeepers who are the record keepers. HR professionals must understand the difference between assets (what is owned by the organization) and expenses since financial decisions will differ depending on whether the transaction is an asset or an expense.

Scenario One

The company paid $22,000 annual cost of routine repair and maintenance on company equipment.

Expense. It was an ordinary and necessary cost incurred in the acquisition (or installation) of the machine.

Scenario Two

The company paid $412,000 for land, which included title search fees.

Asset. Title search fees are ordinary and necessary costs incurred to acquire land. The buyer needs to be aware of any "clouds" to title (i.e., potential adverse claims).

Scenario Three

$11,500 was paid to repair the company building roof after a hail storm.

Expense. This is a repair expense, and the monies paid do not extend the life of the building so there is no asset addition.

Change Steward

For a true change to occur throughout the HR profession there must first be a paradigm shift in which human resources is a strategic instead of a tactical decision maker. With more knowledge comes more power, as was discussed earlier. As individual members of human resources get onboard with knowing and understanding the complex financial aspects of their organization, they can become mentors to those who are not sure where to begin or how to use their new-found financial intelligence.

The days when HR professionals were unable or unwilling to analyze financial statements, budgets, or ratios will be gone, and this sweeping change could influence those in non-management positions to also move up the organization by obtaining more business literacy. Leading by example is a well-known and accepted way to help others within an organization to realize their potential.

What You Should Know

- The goal of financial accounting is the creation of the financial statements.

- The types of accounts used to record financial transactions, which will ultimately be part of the financial statements, are assets, liabilities, capital, revenue, expenses, and withdrawals/dividends.

- Financial statements are interconnected because the final number of one statement flows down to the other.

- Income statements are always done first, and net income flows down to the statement of owners' equity.

- The statement of owners' equity tells the owner how much is invested (not worth) in the business.

- The ending capital from the statement of owners' equity flows down to the balance sheet. The balance sheet must balance and have the assets equal total liabilities and capital (equity).

- The statement of cash flows often stands alone, but the first line of the statement is net income, which comes from the income statements.

CHAPTER 4

Multiple Facets and Approaches to the Financials

The financial aspect of any organization, whether it is a for-profit or a not-for-profit entity, can be multi-faceted. The perspective and level of information required about the financials of an organization depends on the needs of the users. For example, shareholders seek information about earnings, while customers are more interested in the longevity of the company—especially if they expect to remain loyal customers.

Not all individuals inside or outside an organization need to know specific financial information, but we believe that all employees should understand the general financial strengths and weaknesses of the company where they are employed. Job security is paramount, and who wants to stay with a company that may not be around 6 or 12 months from now?

Drill Down

Businesses rarely make decisions based on superficial information. Instead, they perform what is known as due diligence, or an in-depth fact-finding mission. Drilling down into the specific nature and causes of a situation will help the decision maker feel more confident in his or her assessment of the issue.

As Joseph Badaracco suggests in his book *Leading Quietly*, doing the right thing can sometimes involve obtaining an in-depth knowledge of both technological and bureaucratic complexities.[1]

In other words, don't simply analyze business situations superficially.

Badaracco also suggests that leaders never let complexities obscure responsibilities. And don't go it alone, he says. Many business situations were caused by and should be handled by more than one individual at a time. Lastly, he recommends not being hesitant to back off when the situation is beyond one's scope of understanding. When an individual cannot describe a situation or issue in plain language it is a warning sign that the situation is overly complex and additional assistance by others may be warranted.

The moral of the story, especially as it pertains to human resources, is to ask questions!

Look at the Income Statement First

There are key strategies that can be followed that allow for a more effective way to interpret the financial statements. First, look at the income statement. Although an income statement shows less than most people realize, it is a great place to start because the "bottom line" is net income or, worst case, net loss. If there is a consistent pattern of net income instead of net loss, that tells you that the organization is doing a decent job of managing costs compared to the revenue from the same time period.

Income Statements and HR

The expense side as opposed to the revenue side of the business usually applies to human resources. Typically, accounting rules use the accrual method, meaning that whether or not the expenses have already been paid, they are listed as expenses (more on this in chapter 5). The expenses that would be under the control or purview of human resources could include salaries, bonuses, payroll taxes, commissions, and training expenses.

Before we discuss an organization-wide income statement, let us take a look at a partial income statement that relates directly to the HR professional. Keep in mind that income statements are rarely, if ever, developed on a departmental level. Instead, there is more of a reliance on departmental budgets (see chapter 8). Income statements are developed for the entire organization, but this example shows the basics with which the HR department would be familiar.

Alpha Company Income Statement
HR DEPT DRAFT

Sales Revenue	$ 345,000
Less Expenses:	
Recruiting Expense	($ 10,000)
Bad Debt Expense	($ 48,000)
Payroll Expense	($ 78,000)
Net Income	$ 209,000

What you have above is sales revenue less expenses. The bottom line is net income. In this case, the net income is $209,000. The only way to know if this is good or bad is to compare your department budget to your actual numbers. Some expenses relate directly and without question to a particular department, whereas other expenses—such as overhead expenses—are allocated to your department.

Overhead Expenses

Overhead expenses are expenses that exist regardless of how much or how little the company earns in terms of sales of either products or services. These expenses are like dead-weight, or a necessary evil.

For example, let's say that the annual expense for the corporate office is $100,000 and there are 10 departments using equal percentages of the square footage of the building. Each department could be allocated the expense on their department level budget of $10,000 (10 percent of the total $100,000).

Trend Analysis

Trend analysis is a pattern of numbers over several years. One year of financial information is insufficient for decision making since there is no pattern. Trend analysis is a very powerful tool, and on the following page we show examples of both common sizing analysis and horizontal analysis.

The reason trend analysis is so critical is that when changes in numbers are graphed, anyone can step back and see a pattern over time. For example, if recruiting expenses are consistently low but sales are trending upwards, one might question why more employees are not being recruited for future sales and company growth.

Types of Trend Analysis

Common Sizing Financial Statement Analysis. When accounts from a particular financial statement are grouped and shown as a percentage of either total assets in a balance sheet—or—percentage of sales for an income statement.

Horizontal Analysis. When each account on the financial statement is shown as a percentage change from the previous year.

Trend Analysis as an Integral Aspect of Strategy Architect Competency

There are numerous quantitative and qualitative methods to use to assess an organization's strengths and weaknesses (internal assessment) along with its externally focused opportunities and threats. One easy-to-use but powerful quantitative method is trend analysis. Knowing how the organization has performed over the past few years gives all levels of management much-needed information to make the best possible decisions for the future.

Management often conducts comparative financial statement analysis by analyzing several consecutive balance sheets, income statements, or statements of cash flow from year to year.

Trends can be analyzed in the following ways:

- *Direction Example.* Are sales increasing over the last few years or are they decreasing?
- *Speed Example.* Are sales increasing more or less than the associated expenses?

- *Extent Example.* Is rent expense increasing by 10 percent every year or is it holding steady?
- *Trends Example.* Are accounts receivable increasing 15 percent but sales (which generate these accounts receivable, the amount owed to the business by its customers) increasing only 5 percent?

Common Sizing Vertical Trend Analysis

The expenses are shown in their actual totals and as a percentage of sales. This vertical analysis shows all employees how expenses change in relation to changes in sales revenue. There are two steps to calculating the percentages:

Step One. Divide each individual item on the income statement into the sales revenue. For example, for 2010 the recruiting expense is $10,000 and revenue is $345,000.

$10,000/$345,000 = 2.90 percent

Step Two. Continue this process until all items on the income statement have been accounted for and they are shown as a percentage of sales revenue (note: "sales" and "sales revenue" are the same thing).

The trend, or pattern of expenses, is critical. Here is an example of what you might see. The results are mixed.

Alpha Company Income Statement

	2010		2009	
Revenue	$ 345,000	100.00%	$ 421,000	100.00%
Recruiting Expense	$ 10,000	2.90%	$ 10,000	2.38%
Sales Commissions	$ 48,000	13.91%	$ 46,000	10.93%
Payroll	$ 78,000	22.61%	$ 78,000	18.53%
Net Income	$ 209,000	60.58%	$ 287,000	68.17%

Let's analyze this from a business instead of a purely HR perspective: Sales commissions should move in an identical fashion as sales since commissions are normally tied to sales revenue. The year 2010 had lower sales, but as a percentage of sales, commissions went from approximately 11 percent to almost 14 percent. This is a red flag.

What about overall net income? Sales went down substantially from the prior year. However, many of the expenses are fixed and not variable, so the bottom line, again, as a percentage of sales is not as bad as could be expected. Net income for 2010 is nearly 61 percent of sales, only an 8 percent drop in net income from 2009.

Horizontal Trend Analysis

	2009	2008	Change	Change %
Sales	$123,900	$142,876	(18,976)	-13.3%
Cost of goods sold	$34,788	$45,099	(10,311)	-22.9%
Gross profit (Margin)	$89,112	$97,777	(8,665)	-8.9%
Operating expenses				
Selling, general and administrative	$31,877	$37,666	(5,789)	-15.4%
Supplies expense	$7,855	$6,744	1,111	16.5%
Miscellaneous expenses	$1,344	$1,290	54	4.2%
Earnings from operations	$48,036	$52,077		
Interest expense	$997	$967	30	3.1%
Earnings before income taxes	$47,039	$51,110	(4,071)	-8.0%
Provision for income taxes	$8,524	$8,081	443	5.5%
Net earnings	$38,515	$43,029	(4,514)	-10.5%

In horizontal trend analysis, percentage change is calculated. This means that the amount two numbers changed by from one year to the next is stated as a percentage. For example, if training fees were $10,000 last year and are $11,000 this year, the change is $1,000 and the percentage change is 10 percent. One would expect line items on the financials to change approximately by the same percentages. This is because changes in one aspect of the financials are normally tied to changes in another. For example, if sales increased by 20 percent from last year to this year, one would expect many expenses to change by about the same percentage since it costs money to make money. Inventory would have to go up about 20 percent since the company would not want to run out of product.

In this trend analysis, sales decreased approximately 13 percent between 2008 and 2009. We would then look to see if the cost of goods sold (COGS) decreased by the same or higher percentage. In this case, COGS decreased almost 23 percent, which means that the company did an even better job controlling costs in 2009 than it did in 2008.

Each line item is analyzed for percentage change and compared to the percentage that sales decreased. One would expect that expenses would also decrease approximately 13 percent, the same as sales decreased. For the most part, the expenses were on target, but note that the supplies expense increased disproportionately. This would be acceptable if there is a valid reason for the high supplies expense in the current year.

Why Would HR Use Trend Analysis?

Our hypothetical HR manager, Meggan Logan, is becoming increasingly well-informed about the business decisions made within her organization. She currently is analyzing a comparative income statement in order to know the trend in profitability over the past two years.

The example of her company's actual numbers are shown on the spreadsheet on the next page.

Important Trends: Management's Calculations

Comparative Income Statement Example

	1998	1997	Change in Millions	Change %
Sales	$13,406	$14,538	(1,132)	-7.8%
Cost of goods sold	$7,293	$7,976	(683)	-8.6%
Gross profit	$6,113	$6,562	(449)	-6.8%
Operating expenses				
Selling, general and administrative	$3,303	$3,912	(609)	-15.6%
Research and development	$922	$1,230	(308)	-25.0%
Restructuring costs	0	$1,290	(1,290)	-100.0%
Interest expense	$110	$98	12	12.2%
Other income	$328	$21	307	1461.9%
Earnings before income taxes	$2,106	$53	2,053	3873.6%
Provision for income taxes	$716	$48	668	1391.7%
Net earnings	$1,390	$5	1,385	27700.0%

Let's see what Meggan sees and help her develop some valuable input for her peers in management.

- The comparative years are 1997 as the numbers changed in 1998. Percentage change calculations level the playing field and make comparisons more meaningful.

- Sales decreased by almost 8 percent, but gross profit decreased by only about 7 percent so she knows that the costs of the inventory sold to customers did not increase that much. Good news.

- Research and development costs went down, and that could be good or bad depending on the long-term plans for development of new products or services.

- Interest expense increased by over 12 percent, so new debt could have been incurred.

- Other income jumped by a substantial amount, so she would need some details about how and why this occurred.

- Income taxes also increased, but that is acceptable since net income increased.

What can Meggan assess from this information? First, although sales decreased from one year to the next, gross profit did not decrease as much as expected. Second, there was no large restructuring cost, which is good news. Restructuring costs could have stemmed from a merger or acquisition. Third, selling and administrative costs decreased more than sales decreased, so this is a good situation at least in the short run. An increase in interest expense could mean there is a new loan to purchase more inventory for sale, so it could mean higher potential sales in year three. There are instances in which institutional investors force a poorly performing company to restructure.[2]

The net income rolls over into the statement of owners' equity if the organization is a sole proprietorship (i.e., has one owner), or to the "statement of retained earnings" if the organization is a corporation. Rolling over simply means that the end result of one financial statement becomes an integral part of the next financial statement; without the end result, the next financial statement will not be complete or accurate.

SWOT Analysis as a Part of Strategy Architect Competency

As discussed in chapter 1, one aspect of the Strategy Architect competency is being able to develop and interpret the strengths, weaknesses, opportunities, and threats (SWOT) analysis. When human resources can be an unbiased strategic partner and decision maker, all levels and layers of management can benefit from something like SWOT analysis.

SWOT analysis has two levels: internal and external. The first two aspects of strengths and weaknesses of the organization are internally focused and are within the control of the organization, whereas the opportunities and threats facing the organization cannot be controlled to any true extent by management and are macro environmental issues. SWOT analysis can be quantitative and/or qualitative.

SWOT analysis is only a starting place for an organization to identify areas on which it needs to focus. When human resources possesses the necessary business literacy levels required to make financially sound decisions, then human resources becomes more credible in the aspect of the Strategy Architect competency.

Know What Detail Is Missing

There are condensed financial statements, and there are multi-step financial statements. The level of detail is contingent upon the needs of the reader. The examples we see in this survival guide are more on the simplistic side. In Appendix E you will see some more-complex examples of financial statements. I suggest you take a quick look at the more-complex, detailed financial statements so you are familiar with their format and some of the line items that can appear on the statements.

Statement of Cash Flow

We discuss the statement of cash flows separately because it is more complex than the other financial statements. We devote a large portion of a chapter on its discussion.

We talked about the fact that many companies cease to exist because they are not able to manage their most important asset: cash.

See Appendix A to see how a surveyed group fared on the question of the main purpose of the cash flow statement. The survey respondents did very well with this question. The answer is: The primary goal of the statement of cash flows is to calculate the many components of what makes cash increase and decrease.

In its most basic terms, the statement of cash flows consists of the numerous items that either increase or decrease cash. Sounds simple doesn't it? That could not be further from the truth. There is much confusion on many levels of management when it comes to understanding the statement of cash flows. For that reason, we have an entire chapter devoted to explaining some of the basics and interpretations of this important financial statement. But we are going to make sure that after you read chapter 6 you are much more comfortable with the statement of cash flows.

Activity Based Costing

Activity based costing (ABC) systems require the business to identify key or fundamental activities that cause costs to be incurred. These activities are cost drivers.

Activity based accounting theory states that activities can be tracked and these costs would not exist without certain activities being part of the business process of producing goods and services. It is a more time-consuming way of monitoring costs of a particular job or project, but the productivity of both assets and employees can be more consistently analyzed.

Examples of cost drivers include machine setups, materials handling activities, quality inspection, sales order preparation, etc. Cost drivers that relate directly to human resources might include the multiple steps involved in recruiting. These cost drivers would include direct mailings and telephone calls involved in recruiting and hiring new employees. The company owner or management must decide ahead of time what each activity cost will be.

What is needed to calculate ABC?

- The number of times each activity will be performed per year
- The cost of each activity

These activity based costs are then applied to products. This system is in contrast to the traditional cost method of applying overhead via direct labor hours or machine hours.

Advantages

- ABC is more accurate in tracking costs of performing a service or developing a product
- Management is more aware of the cause and effect that lead to the incurrence of costs.

Disadvantages

It is much more time-consuming to track all these different costs caused by activities in the production of goods and services.

Example of Activity Based Costing

	time in hours	per hour	cost to the business for this activity
Order processing	0.2	$20	$4
Transportation to client	0.9	$28	$25
Lawn moving	1.2	$32	$38
Shrub trimming	0.3	$19	$6
Total cost per job			$73

For each of the costs, the fraction of an hour is multiplied by the cost per hour to equal the last column to the right, which is "cost to the business for this activity." Once these per-hour costs are established for each activity, the total cost per job can be calculated.

Again, remember that there are opportunity costs with spending this much time tracking costs. Perhaps the organization would be better off spending its time in enhanced marketing efforts instead of cost-tracking efforts.

Today, employees are asked to create more value with fewer resources, with the exception of the heavy reliance on software packages. Companies may be able to glean some knowledge from CPA firms and some law firms that monitor and measure employees' time spent on specific clients' audits or tax returns. Hours are often represented in 1/10th of an hour or in six-minute intervals.

Relevance and Reliability

These are the two primary qualities of accounting information, and their importance should be noted. When information, accounting or otherwise, is relevant it can affect a decision. It can be relevant to the user in that it can help predict future outcomes and have predictive value.

So, how does that help human resources? Knowing that the financial information can have both predictive and feedback value can help human resources see that there are a couple of different ways to see the same information depending on the needs of the decision maker.

Reliability means that the information is credible or believable. Reliable information is verifiable so that different people viewing the same information will conclude the same things.

Disclosure and Consistency

Companies that are publicly traded must disclose (explain) the financial numbers in paragraph form at the end of the annual report. This is done so there are no secrets between the company and the investors.

Companies must report their financial transactions similarly from year to year without changing the rules or the approach that they use. Consistency means comparability from one year to the next, and investors can understand and compare one year's balance sheet to the next year's more easily when the company adheres to this principle.

How Disclosure and Consistency Principles Relate to HR

It is important for HR professionals to realize that *if* their company is publicly traded, the disclosure requirements are quite steep and specific per the Securities and Exchange Commission. Publicly traded companies are scrutinized to a great extent. Human resources can find out more about its organization's financials by reading the disclosure notes (also called footnotes) at the end of the annual report.

Human resources can also benefit from knowing that the financials must follow similar format and rules of reporting financial transactions from year to year. It is easier to compare apples to apples than apples to oranges, as the saying goes.

Financial Statements: Not Telling the Whole Story

There are several reasons why financial statements do *not* tell the whole story. Here are some examples.

Financial statements reflect past events, not future events of the business. They are not forward-thinking. Therefore, there are information lags wherein the event occurred (i.e., sales) and it was recorded up to a year later if the organization creates income statements annually vs. quarterly.

Also, accountants and finance managers have an on-going disagreement about how assets should be recorded on the balance sheet. Accountants focus on reliability of source documents and maintain that the original costs are reflected on the original document. Finance managers focus more on revaluation of assets to reflect their current values because they are more concerned with the relevance of the numbers rather than reliable sources that are not subject to bias. Although this theoretical difference still exits, financial statements are still based on historical information, not current information. That means that the assets on the balance sheet could actually be worth more or less than their original cost, but accountants do *not* adjust the values of the assets on the balance sheet as conditions change.

Taxes: Why the HR Professional Should Care

Corporate taxes play a key role in strategic planning and strategic management of an organization. Decisions made by management often have to be analyzed from a tax perspective since they have tax ramifications. For our purposes, we will focus on the taxes that apply to HR's role—primarily payroll taxes.

Tax Responsibilities of the Organization

- *FICA Social Security*—companies match (pay half of) their W-2 employees' withholding. 6.2 percent of the employees' paycheck must be paid by both the employee and the employer. There is a cap or max above which no tax must be withheld.

- *Medicare*—companies also match and both employers and employees pay 1.45 percent of their W-2 employees' salaries. There is no minimum or maximum in earnings for this tax, so regardless of how much an employee makes, this 1.45 percent is withheld.

- *Unemployment Insurance*—typically companies pay this tax on behalf of their employees, but some states and companies are having their employees pay a small share of this tax.

It would be an easy argument to associate the Operational Executor competency with payroll and payroll taxes since human resources is involved with setting up, managing, or monitoring payroll. But do these members of human resources really understand some of the behind-the-scenes information that relate to employee tax withholding?

Employee Business Taxes

Many organizations carefully consider whether some or all of their employees can be considered independent contractors or consultants. The IRS has specific rules on this decision (see textbox below). This is important for human resources to understand because employees will either be W-2 employees or independent consultants. This relationship must be clearly defined for new hires. The "degree of control and independence" relates to the degree to which the organization can direct the employee's or contractor/consultant's daily work activities. For example, can the organization dictate if the employee or contractor/consultant uses the organization's resources or works from home? There are ramifications of this decision relating to employee benefits (or lack thereof) and payroll taxes that may be the responsibility of the organization. For example, human resources would have to understand the degree to which the organization can dictate or control how and where the worker performs the task, being careful not to overstep any legal boundaries. On the financial aspect, if the worker is not a W-2 employee, the organization (i.e., human resources) does not control how the worker manages his or her financial aspect of the work being done. Lastly, for the type of relationship, human resources needs to know whether or not the worker is a temporary worker who will not receive benefits and if there are any written contracts with the worker. If the worker is determined to be a contractor, the organization has much less control over how, when, and where the work is completed as compared to the worker being a W-2 employee.

The Merit Rating and How It Affects the Organization

Human resources is typically tasked with communicating to employees when they are being laid off or fired. There are numerous financial ramifications to both the employee and the employer during and immediately following this transition. Some of the financial concerns are vacation pay, severance pay, possible unemployment compensation and

---

Before you can determine how to treat payments you make for services, you must know the business relationship that exists between you and the person performing the services. The person performing the services may be

- An independent contractor
- An employee (common-law employee)
- A statutory employee
- A statutory nonemployee

In determining whether the person providing service is an employee or an independent contractor, all information that provides evidence of the degree of control and independence must be considered.

Independent Consultant Classification vs. W-2 Employee

When an organization hires new employees or contracts with contractors, human resources needs to know the tax responsibilities of the organization and of the individual with whom they are negotiating (see the table below). The following table summarizes the basic characteristics that differentiate W-2 employees from independent contractors/consultants. Before human resources proceeds through the hiring process, this decision has to be made. Specifically, does the organization want to hire someone who is independent and will work on their own terms, or does it want to undertake the financial responsibility of paying part of the W-2 employee's Social Security taxes and other benefits?

Independent Consultants/1099 Consultants	W-2 Employees
Often considered temporary or project based	Paid employee benefits in most cases
Not paid employee benefits	Pay half of their own Social Security FICA and Medicare and the employer pays the other half
Pay their own Social Security FICA and Medicare themselves with no monies paid on their behalf by the organization	

---

potential legal issues depending on the circumstances for the layoff.

Human resources typically does not see the accounting or financial side of this employee downsizing decision. Depending on the state in which the company does business, there are some state unemployment penalties for too many layoffs within a certain timeframe. The merit rating is a reflection of the number and frequency of employee layoffs.

When making an offer to a prospective independent consultant, the HR professional should be aware that from the individual's perspective there are advantages and disadvantages compared to being a W-2 employee.

Advantage

1099 consultants can deduct employee business expenses from the 1099 income and report both the income and the deductions on Schedule C. Appendix C provides an example of a Form 1099 that would be issued to independent contractors/consultants at the end of the year.

Disadvantage

1099 consultants must pay their entire Social Security tax themselves, and sometimes individuals are unaware of this requirement unless human resources informs them of it.

Common-Law Rules

Common-law rules are established through custom and precedent, especially court-case precedent. Common law varies by state and municipality.

Facts that provide evidence of the degree of control and independence fall into three categories:

1. Behavioral: Does the company control or have the right to control what the worker does and how the worker does his or her job?

2. Financial: Are the business aspects of the worker's job controlled by the payer? (these include things like how the worker is paid, whether expenses are reimbursed, who provides tools/supplies, etc.)

3. Type of Relationship: Are there written contracts or employee-type benefits (i.e., pension plan, insurance, vacation pay, etc.)? Will the relationship continue, and is the work performed a key aspect of the business?

Source: "Independent Contractor (Self-Employed) or Employee?" IRS.gov. Available at www.irs. gov/businesses/small/article/0,,id=99921,00.html.]

In effect, companies with poor merit ratings pay higher levels of unemployment insurance.

Unemployment insurance rate increases can affect the bottom line of an organization. There is a direct correlation between the level and frequency of layoffs and the dollar amounts of unemployment insurance that is paid.

As mentioned in the previous textbox table, 1099 consultants must pay their entire FICA and Medicare themselves.

Not having the employer pay half of this tax obligation is often not discussed with potential 1099 consultants. These two taxes, when paid solely by the individual, add up to just under 15 percent of net income. The net income would be the same as the income earned only if there are no out-of-pocket business expenses paid by the employee. Otherwise, the net income would be lower than what is reported and earned by the employee.

Social Responsibility

But profit is not always the only goal. Many organizations also balance their goal of profit-seeking with giving back to the community. This is where social responsibility comes in. Companies may try to incorporate some social responsibility or giving back to their community in numerous ways. Examples may include charitable giving, sponsoring the local baseball team, or encouraging their employees to volunteer their time to local charities.

Companies often seek ways to enhance their reputation in their community or state. In the long run, this can often result in higher sales since potential customers may have a more favorable impression of companies that promote goals other than financial goals.

What You Should Know

- Don't look at any aspect of the financials superficially.
- Look at the income statement first.
- Human resources affects, and is affected by, the "bottom line."

- Trend analysis is important because financial trends tell a story and show a pattern. It is better to have several years of financial statements rather than just one year; a trend can tell management the direction sales and individual expenses are going.

- Trend analysis is a key aspect of the Strategy Architect competency.

- Focusing on the statement of cash flows is important in understanding how cash is spent or collected by the organization. Cash is critical.

- Human resources needs to ask what allocation method is used to "push" part of overhead costs into department budgets. The allocation method must make sense for that type of organization and must be applied consistently.

- Sometimes, the financial statements do not tell the whole story because they are a summary of past events and use original costs vs. current costs.

- Human resources must be aware of the important differences between W-2 employees and independent contractors/consultants. There are financial responsibilities, such as benefits and tax obligations, associated with W-2 employees.

CHAPTER 5

Financial Results May Differ: Accrual vs. Cash Basis

This concept of accrual versus cash basis financial reporting is simple on its surface, but the ramifications of whether an organization uses the cash or accrual basis of accounting can be quite complex. This relates to the seventh competency of business literacy discussed in chapter 2 since individuals who can interpret financial decisions are more credible and part of the decision making team within an organization.

Accrual and Cash Basis Financial Reporting

Accrual basis accounting is the preferred method, although some organizations use cash basis financial reporting. Publicly traded and larger companies are required to use accrual based accounting. Typically only very small or closely held (owned) companies use the cash basis.

Fundamentally, accrual accounting records financial transactions regardless of when cash changes hands. So, revenue that has been earned is recorded (recognized by the organization) even if the customers do not pay in the current period. Cash basis is less accurate because transactions such as revenue and expenses are ignored until cash changes hands. Cash basis often distorts what is happening within an organization since it is overly dependent on the timing of cash being received or paid by the organization for recording the transaction.

Scenario

Alpha Company uses the accrual method of accounting. Dunno Nuttin Company uses the cash basis method of bookkeeping. Let's see how the results can differ substantially based on the method chosen.

Can you, the HR professional, make an accurate comparison of these two companies using different recording techniques? Below you will see both an income statement and a balance sheet for both companies.

Alpha Company Balance Sheet
31-Dec-10

Cash	$45,000	Liabilities:	
Accounts Receivable	$39,000	Accounts Payable	$46,700
Equipment	$80,000	Capital	$117,300
Total Assets	$164,000	Total Liabilities and Capital	$164,000

Dunno Nuttin' Company Balance Sheet
31-Dec-10

Cash	$90,000		
Supplies	$4,000		
Equipment	$45,000	Capital	$139,000
Total Assets	$139,000	Total Liabilities and Capital	$139,000

Let's look at the primary differences.

First, what is missing in the Dunno Nuttin Company's balance sheet? It is using the cash method, which means that *only* transactions that have been settled with cash are recorded. Therefore, there would be no accounts receivable, which is the money owed to the company in the near future. There would also be no accounts payable, which are the monies owed to other businesses for everything from a telephone bill to purchase of equipment.

The cash basis is much easier to understand, but it is less sophisticated, less accurate, and limited in its usefulness in providing enough information to its users about the financial state of the organization.

According to accounting rules, the accrual basis of accounting better predicts future earnings and receipts of cash receipts and payments.

Advantages of Accrual Basis

• Accrual accounting recognizes revenue as it is *earned* rather than waiting until cash is *received* for the revenue earned.

• Accrual accounting more accurately reflects revenue and expenses in the correct year

• Cash flow is more volatile than income.

Disadvantages of Accrual Basis

• Matching net income and cash flow is no easy task. There is a trade-off between relevance and reliability, and this can be viewed as a type of continuum. (See below.) Cash accounting is more reliable but less relevant, and accrual accounting is more relevant.

Relevance _____ × _____ × _____ Reliability
                        Accrual   Cash
                        Accounting   Accounting

See Appendix A for survey participants' perceptions about the advantages and disadvantages of using accrual over cash basis accounting.

Free Cash Flow

Free cash flow is important to organizations since it signifies what cash is available to the organization at any point in time. This concept does not include details about whether the cash is currently available (such as in a checking account) or unavailable (such as in a CD or other financial instrument). Recall that monitoring levels of cash within an organization is very important since organizations must be able to pay both their short- and long-term financial obligations.

In this example we will calculate the cash flow for Alpha Company. We start with reported earnings (cash inflow) and then make adjustments to get free cash flow.

Earnings before depreciation and taxes	$2,630,000
Depreciation (noncash expense)	$ (80,000)
Earnings before taxes	$2,550,000
Taxes (cash outflow)	$ (484,500)
Earnings after taxes	$2,065,500
Depreciation	$ 80,000
Cash flow	$2,145,500

Let's list how some typical business situations affect income and free cash flow.

How Certain Transactions Affect Free Cash Flow

Transaction	Income Effect	Free Cash Flow Effect
Sales on credit (Accounts Receivable)	increase	none
Cash collected from Accounts Receivable	none	increase
Cash purchase of equipment	none	decrease

This leads us to the next topic about accrual accounting requiring judgment and various estimations.

Estimates

HR professionals should be aware that accounting is not always an exact science and that there are estimates involved. Estimates are not wild guesses in accounting. They are based on historical data or industry practices. For example, depreciation expenses are based on assumptions about the length of time it should take to gradually write off the expense of equipment or a building. Another example is accounts receivable mentioned above. HR professionals need to recognize the possibility that not all of the company's customers will pay their bills to the company, thereby allowing for the possibility that sales do not equal cash in hand. Some of these customers could pay late. As a result, cash management gets more complicated as the inflow and outflow of cash may not coincide.

Accruals and HR

Below you will see several examples of accruals. Vacation benefits and payroll taxes accruals relate directly to human resources. It is important for human resources to be familiar with accruals because accruals accurately reflect some financial items that accrue, or increase over time.

Vacation Benefits

Organizations typically accrue (account for and estimate) their employees' vacation benefit expense. This may sound unnecessary because when a full-time employee uses his or her vacation time, there is no extra expense to the organization. It makes sense in accounting terms since the benefit is an expense to the organization. No products or services have been provided by the employee to the organization during this vacation time used.

Payroll Taxes Accrual

There are always differences between estimated taxes per the organization's tax return and its income statement. There is also a timing difference between when taxes are withheld from employees' paychecks and when the monies are remitted to the appropriate tax authority.

Depreciation

This is the writing off of the cost of an asset over its estimated useful life. Writing off means deducting part of the expense of an asset every year on the income statement until it is fully deducted (i.e., written off). An example would be an asset like equipment, the cost of which would be deducted gradually over the course of a number of years. It has nothing to do with the value of the asset decreasing over time, as is commonly thought. Depreciation expense is taken every year on the income statement until an asset is fully depreciated. It does not mean that the asset has to be sold or discarded after it is fully depreciated. Rather, it means that the organization wants to match the revenue generated by the use of the asset owned and the associated depreciation, or gradual write off of the asset.

Companies often use either straight line or double declining depreciation to write off the costs of their tangible assets.

Straight line depreciation is the easiest type of depreciation method to use since the same depreciation expense amount is used every year that is applicable, until the asset is fully depreciated.

See the example:

On January 1, 2011, Casey's Taxi Company purchased a new cab for $20,000. The estimated salvage value (value of the asset at the end of its life) of the cab is $2,000, and the cab's useful life is to be 10 years.

The basic formula is: Depreciation expense equals the cost (of the asset) minus the salvage value/estimated useful life.

As calculated:

Depreciation expense = $20,000-$2,000/10 yrs = $1,800 per year for each of these ten years.

Accumulated depreciation is a contra asset, and I like to describe it as filling a cup. Each year the layers fill up toward the top. This holding area/cup/accumulation of depreciation fills up by the end of the useful life (i.e., typically number of years, although it could be stated in months).

Here is a segment of how the depreciable equipment is shown on the asset side of the balance sheet after one year:

Equipment	$20,000
Less: Accumulated Depreciation	($1,800)
Book Value	$ 18,200

Double declining balance/declining balance (DDB) is more complex and is considered to be an accelerated depreciation method. Accelerated method means that in the early years of the life of the asset more depreciation expense is taken, and in the later years less depreciation expense is taken. It is calculated differently from the straight line method, and each year the dollar amounts of depreciation expense will differ.

Why should a company use DDB rather than the straight line method? Because higher depreciation expense on the income statement equates to lower net income and lower taxes, at least in the first years of the asset's life.

By way of example, let's use the same scenario and numbers used above for the straight line method example.

On January 1, 2011, Casey's Taxi Company purchased a new cab for $20,000. The estimated salvage value of the cab is $2,000, and the cab's useful life is to be 10 years. Calculate using DDB method of depreciation.

The calculation:

Year one: $20,000 x 20% = $4,000 depreciation expense

Year two: ($20,000 – $ 4,000) x 20% = $3,200 depreciation expense

Interest Expense

Organizations can raise capital (money) by incurring debt and/or selling bonds. The cost to the organization for either type of debt is interest. When organizations use the accrual method of accounting, this interest expense must be accrued or estimated. There must be matching between the interest expense and its benefit period. One cannot wait until the debt is mature to consider this cost to the organization.

Warranty Expense

Warranties must be estimated or accrued for by organizations since the expense of the possible warranty expense must be matched with the revenue earned from sale of that product. For example, in 2010 Toyota most likely underestimated its warranty liability since it had the acceleration pedal fiasco in which thousands of cars had to be repaired or at least inspected. It probably underestimated its financial warranty responsibility to its customers. Regardless of the level of warranties that get exercised (used when a customer comes back to get a product serviced or replaced), most organizations need to anticipate or accrue for this expense.

In this scenario, sales were $7 million. Based on prior years' experiences, the company anticipates that 0.5 percent of sales must be accrued for warranty expenses. There is already a beginning balance of $46,000 in the estimated warranty liability account, and the actual expense paid to customers for warranty repairs is $31,200.

Warranty Expense =

($7,000,000 sales x 0.5% estimated warranty expense) =	$35,000
Estimated Warranty Liability, 1/1/09 balance	$46,000
Less: Actual warranty costs during 2009	$(31,200)
Add: Warranty Expense accrued during 2009	$35,000
Estimated Warranty Liability, 12/31/09 balance	$49,800

The bottom line: accrual accounting involves recognizing liabilities before they are paid.

Overlooking an Accrual

ABC Company's accountant failed to accrue as of December 31, 2010, some employee fringe benefit program expenses that were incurred in 2010 and that will be paid in 2011. The result of this omission is to understate 2010 expenses and current liabilities as of December 31, 2010. Current liabilities are liabilities that will be paid in one year or less. The reason that the current liabilities would be underestimated/understated at the end of 2010 is that these employee benefits would actually be paid in 2011.

What You Should Know

- Accrual based accounting is more relevant than cash basis bookkeeping, and it records transactions regardless of when cash changes hands.

- Accrual accounting is designed to match revenues and expenses and has nothing to do with cash changing hands.

- Accrual accounting more accurately reflects the financial transactions of the organization, but it is more complex and requires a more thorough understanding of accounting.

- Accounting often consists of estimates that should be made based on reasonable assumptions. Examples of estimates include employee vacation benefits, depreciation, and warranty expenses.

- Depreciating a tangible asset means writing off the cost of the asset gradually. The straight line method is the simplest method, but the double declining method is often used by organizations.

- Overlooking an accrual distorts the financials.

CHAPTER 6

Cash Equals Financial Survival

This chapter is made up of various topics, including bankruptcies and restructuring, cash management, and the statement of cash flows. We emphasize the statement of cash flows to a great extent because interpreting it is critical for management of all levels.

Business Ally Competency and Cash Management

The Business Ally competency was first introduced in chapter 2. As you may recall, HR professionals who possess this competency understand how their organization makes money, who their customers are, and why their customers are loyal to their organization. Management of all the different functional areas in an organization must have a thorough understanding and working knowledge of the statement of cash flows. HR professionals who are Business Allies are often key players in the financial decision making process. Cash management is one of the most important aspects of effective financial management.

Credit Crunches and Tight Money

Since 2008, the United States has been suffering through a recession exacerbated by a near collapse of the housing market. One of the financial ramifications of this recession has been a severe limitation on bank credit. This credit crunch has manifested itself throughout all aspects of the economy, and no industry or type of organization has gone unaffected.

Many organizations depend not only on long-term loans and credit but also on short-term liquidity loans such as working capital loans. These short-term loans allow for businesses to purchase their inventory to then sell to their customers or to pay their employees in a timely fashion. When credit is severely limited, there is a ripple effect in the economy. The free flow of cash and credit is paramount to growth of organizations and the economy.

Sufficient Cash Is Critical for Financial Survival

One of the primary reasons many companies fail is due to mismanagement or lack of cash. Therefore, it would behoove the HR profession to become very familiar with the statement of cash flow. Perhaps these HR managers could enlighten some of the other departments' managers once the knowledge has been obtained.

Credible Activist Interpreting the Statement of Cash Flows

Recall in chapter 2 when we first introduced the Credible Activist competency for HR professionals. Credible Activists do the right thing at the right time. Managing cash effectively and efficiently can mean the difference between survival and the demise of the organization. When HR professionals fully understand their role in making good financial decisions as they relate to cash management, the entire organization can benefit.

It is important to know that the statement of cash flows was previously called "Sources and Uses of Cash." It is important because the statement of cash flows is the most complex of the four financial statements, but if you remember the phrase "sources and uses" as you calculate it or interpret it, you will have a much easier time. Sources of cash mean an increase in cash, and uses of cash mean a decrease in cash (i.e., like the household budget, the more uses of funds generally means less funds on hand)

Bankruptcies and Reorganizations

In recent years the number of bankruptcies and reorganizations has increased substantially as economic growth has stagnated. Many companies are struggling to stay in business. Some organizations facing financial difficulties are able to temporarily postpone or divert the demise of their business by restructuring and/or downsizing their operations. Human resources is often an integral player during these challenging times.

Bankruptcy Types

There are two common types of bankruptcies that companies can file. The first is called Chapter 7, in which the organization ceases to exist once all claims have been paid. The other is Chapter 11. Chapter 11 may be filed voluntarily or involuntarily by the organization. After the organization has gone through the process, the organization is again a viable business.

Restructuring

Organizations undergoing restructuring often hire or consult with organizational design (OD) experts who can guide management through massive changes. HR professionals may have the opportunity to align their competencies with those of OD professionals in creating a smooth transition to the new organizational structure.

Again, it may behoove human resources to be more proactive than reactive during these organizational changes.

HR as Change Steward During Reorganizations

During massive change, HR professionals can rise to the challenge and illustrate to the rest of the company that they understand both the financial and employee aspects of restructuring or reorganizations. Human resources can and should go beyond their traditional role as the company representative during layoffs. Human resources can be an integral part of decision making during restructuring by offering other members of management some informed suggestions.

Is the organization a first mover, for example? (Recall that this term was defined in chapter 1.) If so, human resources should know the advantages and disadvantages of this strategy. Evaluate the company using a SWOT analysis (as defined in chapter 2). Investigate thoroughly both the internal and external strengths and weaknesses of the organization.

Has the organization developed but not fully implemented a viable strategic plan?

Can human resources suggest a more in-depth analysis of the macro-environment in which the organization operates, including both positive and negative economic, political, legal, technological, and socio-cultural aspects that affect the organization?

Overview of the Statement of Cash Flows

There are three sections of the statement of cash flows: operating, financing, and investing. In the partial statement example below, you will see the top section (the operating section).

The operating section shows how changes in balance sheet accounts such as accounts receivable and accounts payable affect the level of cash within an organization. The operating section is typically the longest of the three sections and contains the day-to-day operating accounts of the organization.

The financing section shows changes in accounts that affect how the organization pays or obtains funding. For example, this section would contain sales of bonds or sales of stock that are sources of capital.

The investing section shows how the organization contracts or grows in size. Items that grow or diminish the size of the organization and simultaneously affect cash include sales or purchases of land, building, and equipment.

What affects human resources? The most likely area of interest for human resources would be the operating section. There you will find the most changes or "sources and uses" of cash affecting daily operations. When customers are not paying the company in a timely fashion, accounts receivable is increasing, thereby decreasing the amount of cash the organization has. With less cash from accounts receivable comes less cash for training or hiring, which affects human resources.

Example: One Section of the Statement of Cash Flow

Cash flows from Operating Activities: in thousands	
Net income	$620
Add (deduct) items not affecting cash:	
Depreciation and amortization expense	120
Accounts receivable decrease	15
Inventory increase	(27)
Accounts payable increase	13
Income tax payable decrease	(5)
Net cash provided by operating activities	$736

Why Net Income Is the First Line of the Statement of Cash Flow

In the statement of cash flows, net income is the starting place because net income is based on accrual accounting. As we discussed in chapter 5, accrual based accounting can result in there being a timing difference between when revenues are earned and when cash is received. The same is true for expenses. Although revenue and expenses should be recognized and recorded in the same period (i.e., the matching concept), expenses may be incurred before or after cash changes hands.

This means that there is often a timing difference between when net income is recognized and when cash receipts and/or payments are made. We can see that this is true in the example above where we show the operating section of the statement.

If the company is in better shape regarding cash (no other aspects are analyzed at this juncture), the change in the balance sheet items are a source of cash (sources of cash are positive numbers).

If the company is in worse shape regarding cash, the change in the balance sheet item is a use of cash.

Remember that "sources of cash" are positive numbers on the statement of cash flows and, conversely, "uses of cash" are negative numbers.

Example of One Company's Statement of Cash Flow

In the following example, you will see how one company spent and increased cash. The example is fairly exaggerated to show the point that some companies are inept at managing their cash flow and have no idea what the statement of cash flow reflects.

You will see that each line item is explained or analyzed at the end of the statement.

Here is an example of a poorly managed company *in relation to cash*:

1. Increase in accounts receivable. These customers owe the company more than last year, so the customers have the cash vs. the company having the cash. Not good.

2. Decrease in accounts payable. The company is paying the bills with cash, which is a necessary evil or part of doing business; strictly in relation to cash management, however, this is a use of cash. Not good.

3. The company is purchasing more supplies. Sure, it might need them, but, again, in relation to cash, this is a use of cash. Not good.

4. Decrease in inventory. Finally, the company has found a source of cash. As more inventory is sold, there is cash coming into the business. Good thing.

5. Bonds sold. In the short run this means an influx or source of cash. However, in the long run the company will have to pay bondholders interest. Mixed bag of good and bad.

6. Dividends paid. The company has to keep its shareholders happy by paying them cash dividends but for cash management, this is not a good thing and is a use of cash.

7. Stock sold is similar to bonds sold. This is one of the key ways a company can grow and raise capital. The main downside is that ownership is now spread out or diluted among more shareholders. Good thing for cash management since it is a source of cash.

8. and 9. relate to the company either contracting in size by selling land, equipment or buildings or growing in size and using cash.

Again, whether these things are good or bad depends on the strategic plan of the organization.

This is not to say the organization wants to pay its bills late and incur late fees and/or penalties. Instead, the organization would pay its obligations right before they are due while simultaneously encouraging or requiring customers to pay their bills to the organization quickly.

Dunno Nuttin Company			
Net Income	$12,000		
OPERATING SECTION			
Increase in Accounts Receivable	$(56,000)	1	
Decrease in Accounts Payable	$(11,000)	2	
Depreciation Expense	$1,000		
Increase in Supplies	$(3,000)	3	
Decrease in Inventory	$7,000	4	
NET CASH PROVIDED (USED) FROM OPERATING			$(50,000)
FINANCING SECTION			
Bonds Sold	$120,000	5	
Dividends Paid	$(13,000)	6	
Stock Sold	$23,000	7	
NET CASH PROVIDED (USED) FROM FINANCING			$130,000
INVESTING SECTION			
Land Purchased	$(49,000)	8	
Building Sold	$459,000	9	
NET CASH PROVIDED (USED) FROM INVESTING			$410,000
NET INCREASE IN CASH			**$490,000**
BEGINNING CASH JANUARY 1, 2010			**$100,000**
ENDING CASH DECEMBER 31, 2010			**$590,000**

What You Should Know

- There is a connection between the Business Ally competency and cash management.

- Effective cash management can mean the difference between a company thriving or not surviving.

- Human resources is often a key player during organizational restructuring and uses the Change Steward competency during reorganizations.

- The Credible Activist competency comes into play with interpretation of the statement of cash flows because a Credible Activist makes the right decisions at the right time. This is more possible when he or she has a working knowledge and understanding of the statement of cash flows.

- The statement of cash flow has three sections: operating, financing, and investing.

- The statement of cash flow's ultimate goal is to explain how cash changed from last year to this year (per last year's balance sheet compared to this year's balance sheet)

- The starting place to begin calculation of the statement of cash flow is a comparative set of balance sheets. Each account is analyzed on how it either was a source or use of cash.

CHAPTER 7

Obtaining Capital: Financing the Company

Human resources should be aware of how their company is owned and obtains its capital. Corporations typically have an easier time raising capital than do sole proprietorships or partnerships. There is often the perception that corporations will have more longevity than the other types of entities. This may not always be the case, but that is the perception.

Companies often sell their stock to institutional investors

> "[b]ecause institutional investors such as pension fund and mutual fund own a large percentage of stock in major U.S. companies, these investors are having more to say about the way publicly owned corporations are managed."[1]

Not all companies have two types of stock. If they only have one type of stock, it would be common stock. Common stock is the most prevalent type of stock sold, and only some companies choose to sell preferred stock as well. Preferred stock is used much less than long-term debt in the capital structure of most manufacturing and merchandising companies. This is due to the fact that on the company's tax return dividends paid on preferred stock are not deductible, but interest on long-term debt is deductible.

Business Organizations: The Basic Differences

There are basic differences between a sole proprietorship, partnership, and corporation. (For more specific information or advice, consult with a CPA or legal counsel.) Human resources should be aware of the fundamental differences between types of organizations because each type of entity has different strengths, weaknesses, and potential longevity. Job security can be affected by the type of entity one works for. There are both fundamental and complex reasons to choose a particular type of business.

Sole proprietorships are the easiest and fastest way to get a business up and running, but the major drawback is unlimited liability. Unlimited liability is a major risk since if the business gets sued and all assets are taken as a result of losing that lawsuit, the party suing the business can then take some or all of the personal assets of the sole proprietor.

What is becoming increasingly popular in today's litigious society is the formation of a limited liability company (LLC). In general, corporations provide limited liability, which is a safeguard for personal assets. There are numerous other aspects, including tax ramifications, of deciding what type of business entity to form.

Sole proprietorships obtain capital from their own resources or from loans. Partnerships have more access to capital since banks often view them as more financially stable than a sole proprietorship.

In addition, partners joining a partnership are almost always required to invest capital or other assets such as land or equipment into the partnership in return for a share of the partnership net income.

Corporations that are publicly traded, meaning their stock is traded in the open market (stock exchanges), have the most access for capital. When shareholders purchase shares of their stock, the investment is part of stockholders' equity as discussed further below.

	Type of Entity		
	Sole Proprietorships	Partnerships	Corporations
Number of Owners	One	Two or more partners	One to an infinite number
Ease of Formation	Easiest	Recommended written partnership agreement	Most difficult and expensive
Advantages	Owner can make all decisions	Synergies between partners and more access to capital than sole proprietorships	Limited liability
Disadvantages	Unlimited liability	Unlimited liability	More government oversight and double taxation

Stockholders'/Owners' Equity

Stockholders'/owners' equity (as seen on the balance sheet) is made up of two main components:

Contributed capital: Common and preferred shareholders purchase of company stock means an influx of cash. In this section of equity on the balance sheet, there may be detailed information including a valuation for par and paid-in-capital in excess of par.

Retained earnings: the current and previous years' net income that has been kept or retained in the business. It is accumulated for potential future expansion of the business and/or to replace assets as they wear out. Retained earnings are not the same as cash.

Related to Stocks

Common Stock: The primary feature of common stock is that these shareholders can vote on important company decisions. They can vote at the annual shareholder meeting or designate a representative to vote on their behalf (known as voting by proxy).

Preferred Stock: The primary feature of preferred stocks is that these shareholders get paid first. There are different characteristics of preferred stock, namely cumulative or non-cumulative and participating or non-participating. These concepts are beyond the scope of this book.

Dividends in Arrears: Preferred shareholders who own cumulative preferred stock are entitled to receive dividends in future years if the company cannot pay them their dividend in the current year.

Par Value: An arbitrary and meaningless value given to the stock in the company's corporate charter.

Cash Dividends: The distribution of company profits. Taxable to the recipient.

Stock Dividends: These are often distributed to shareholders instead of cash dividends. It may appease shareholders who are given shares of the company based on their current ownership percentage.

Debt vs. Equity Ownership

Companies are always seeking ways to find the best balance between debt and equity (stock) ownership. Debt brings the burden and responsibility of paying interest on the debt owed, but more widespread stock ownership can mean loss of control of the organization.

Advantages of Debt

- Interest payments are tax deductible to the company.
- The financial obligation is clearly specified and of a fixed nature (no surprises).
- In an inflationary economy, debt may be paid back with cheaper dollars (the dollars have less purchasing power than when received). This will not always be the case.
- The use of debt, up to a prudent point, may lower the cost of capital to the firm.

Disadvantages of Debt

- Interest and principal payment obligations are set by contract and must be paid regardless of the company's ability to pay.

- Bonds and the agreements or contracts associated with these bonds may place burdensome restrictions on the firm. Bonds are often of a very long-term nature.

- Debt, utilized beyond a given point, may serve as a depressant on outstanding common stock.

Characteristics and Differences Between Common Stock, Preferred Stock, and Bonds

	Common Stock	Preferred Stock	Bonds
Owners control the company	YES	—	—
Requirement to provide return to the owners	—	—	YES
Claims to assets if the company declares bankruptcy	—	—	YES
Highest cost of distribution	YES	—	—
Largest return on investment given to owners/investors	YES	—	—
Highest risk to owners/ investors	YES	—	—
Tax deductible payment (for bonds: interest) to the company	—	—	YES
Payment partially tax exempt to corp. recipient	YES	YES	—

Dividends

Dividends are a distribution of corporate earnings. Stock dividends are shares of stock given to shareholders instead of giving them cash. It can appease the shareholders at least in the short term.

Shareholders who purchase stock immediately before a dividend is declared are not entitled to receive a dividend from the company. The board of directors decides if a dividend will be paid to certain shareholders of record. If there is an insufficient level of retained earnings, no dividend should be paid.

The Importance of Cash Dividends

HR professionals should know that cash dividends are a distribution of earnings to shareholders and that these shareholders can be employees of the company. Human resources should also be aware that stock price appreciation is a major consideration to future and current management who are entitled to receive part of their compensation in the form of stock. Some shareholders purchase a company's stock for its long-term price appreciation potential. Stock is often categorized as either:

- Growth stock, which means long-term appreciation is expected
- Income stock, which is stock that pays a dividend
- Value stock, which means that the stock may be underpriced now and the near term expectation is that its value will increase substantially over time.

Dividends are a mixed blessing to shareholders because dividend recipients must pay income taxes on the monies received. A form 1099-DIV (see Appendix D) is sent by the company to its shareholders, and the shareholder must pay tax on this distribution. The company cannot take a tax deduction for this payment as it does with bond interest payments to bond holders.

Return on Investment: Company Paying Cash or Stock Dividends

As stated above, not all shareholders are interested in receiving a cash dividend from the organization in which they have invested. Shareholders who plan on holding the stock for the long term often see the big picture and would prefer the organization hold onto the retained earnings and reinvest it so the company can expand. The return on investment can be higher for the company than on the individual level; therefore, cash dividends should not be paid in certain circumstances.

Stock Splits Are Interpreted as a Sign of Company Growth

Stock splits are typically orchestrated because the company stock price has reached levels that make it less attractive to many potential investors. The price level is so high that investors will not even consider purchasing the company's stock. Stock splits are often seen as a positive sign that the company stock, hence the company itself, is increasing in value.

A stock dividend or a stock split may be of limited value to a shareholder because the shareholder's proportionate interest (investment) in the company does not change.

Types of Stock Splits

A 2:1 stock split means that one share will be split into two shares For example, a stock that was originally valued at $100 will be split into two shares valued at $50 each. In the short term, this stock split is meaningless to current shareholders but it indicates that the stock prices have increased so dramatically recently that the board of directors wanted to make it more affordable to more investors. Thus, the price goes down per share but the number of shares increases for current shareholders.

Another example is a 3:2 split, which is a bit more complicated to calculate since the values of the stock will often be awkward in values such as $244 (not nice, even numbers). An example of a 3:1 split would be when the original share price is $150 per share. After the split, the $150 share becomes three shares worth $50 each. This is important to all employees who own stock in their company.

Reverse Stock Splits

When reverse stock splits occur, investors and employees within an organization may be concerned since it indicates that the stock price has fallen so dramatically that shares are combined. When this happens, the values of each share increases but the number of shares decreases. This could indicate financial difficulties within the company or lack of investor interest in purchasing these shares.

Horizontal vs. Vertical Integration and the Operational Executor

Horizontal integration results when a company purchases its competition. Vertical integration by contrast is when companies that supply goods and services to the company are obtained by the original company (for example, if McDonalds purchased its supplier of bread and rolls). This can result in lower costs to the company.

As discussed in chapter 2, one of the seven HR competencies is the Operational Executor. In this role, HR professionals can assist other functional areas of the organization in designing and implementing policies and procedures that must be upheld after horizontal or vertical integration occurs. There are often dissimilar cultures and different policies and procedures in different organizations, especially if the organizations vary in size, industry, or geographical location. It is the HR professional's responsibility and opportunity to recognize the depth and breadth of changes needed when horizontal or vertical integration is taking place.

Vertical integration affects both companies because the supplier has been purchased after which it is less challenging for the primary, purchasing company to obtain its supplies at a reasonable price and in a timely fashion. The catch is that purchasing any company such as in vertical integration requires funding.

In horizontal integration, a company purchases one of its competitors. This could affect human resources because there could be a duplication of employees doing similar work in both organizations. This could mean that human resources shifts employees around or conducts a reduction in force. In addition, after a horizontal integration there might be more compliance issues for human resources to become familiar with if and when competition has been reduced. There could be legal issues associated with any dramatic decrease in competition within this industry as a result of this purchase. That is only applicable in rare occasions, but if this issue arises, be sure to consult with appropriate legal counsel.

Role of Synergy in HR

Synergy is the amplification of benefits when two or more individuals work together on a common goal. Synergy can exist after a vertical or horizontal integration since two companies have been combined. Management is typically aware of its benefits but often tends to overestimate the potential synergistic advantages associated with this combining of forces.

Despite its often exaggerated benefits, human resources needs to be aware that synergistic effects can occur when individuals with different backgrounds and work experiences are tasked with coming up with a variety of solutions to problems. After a horizontal or vertical integration, there may be a new combination of employees within the larger organization. Human resources can benefit from partnering with others with stronger backgrounds in financial literacy or who have other strengths.

Going Global

"Factors that influence a U.S. business firm to go overseas are: avoidance of tariffs; lower production and labor costs; usage of superior American technology abroad in such area as oil exploration, mining, and manufacturing; tax advantages such as postponement of U.S. taxes until foreign income is repatriated, lower foreign taxes, and special tax incentives; defensive measures to keep up with competitors going overseas; and the achievement of international diversification. There also is the potential for higher returns than on purely domestic investments."[2]

This is important for the HR professional because human resources engages in the recruiting and hiring of employees who will be assigned to overseas assignments (temporarily or permanently). Human resources must also realize that there are legal and financial barriers to entering foreign markets. There could also be some political unrest in other countries, and the company may have to close some overseas operations.

Risks in Expanding into Overseas Markets

Multi-national companies are subject to some types of risk that domestic companies are not affected by, including political risk and currency risk. Political risk pertains to the risk that the foreign country in which the company also operates may experience political unrest. Companies in these types of potential dangers must create contingency plans on how to deal with political issues. Second, some companies that operate overseas or that own subsidiary companies must also deal with currency risks. Currency risk exists because currency rates change daily and are out of the control of the company. Gains and losses from currency fluctuations are recorded by the company's accountants.

HR professionals are acutely affected when their company initially expands overseas or increases its presence overseas. Human resources would be highly involved in hiring employees who will be moved overseas (thereby becoming expatriates), the expatriates' compensation, and overall talent management.

What You Should Know

- Companies have numerous decisions to make when deciding the best way to finance the organization. Balancing debt and equity (stock) can be challenging, and that balance should be constantly monitored.
- There are numerous advantages and disadvantages of debt.
- Bonds are debt. Bond interest expense is paid to bondholders semi-annually.

- There are two main components of stockholders' equity: contributed capital and retained earnings.

- Stock is equity ownership of the organization. Dividends may or may not be paid to shareholders depending on many things, including dividend policy, the board of directors' strategic plans, and mostly the level of retained earnings available to pay dividends.

- Horizontal and vertical integration relate to either purchasing a company's competition or purchasing a supplier.

CHAPTER 8

Budgeting and the HR Professional

To understand the budgeting process, first become more familiar with the primary financial statements (i.e., the balance sheet and the income statement).

There are many instances in which HR professionals can be tasked with developing and/or complying with their organization's budget. Budgets are beneficial because they

- help people make educated assumptions about upcoming expenses;
- allow management to gauge performance;
- provide a benchmark for judging performance;
- require planning by management; and
- require bringing together the functional areas of the company.

On a strategic level, budgets can be developed either with a top down approach wherein there is little or no input from levels of management, or with a participative approach where numerous individuals are involved in the budgeting process. This latter approach creates an attitude supportive of achieving organizational goals.

Budgets are often associated with some negative connotations. Budgets can either be strong suggestions or require mandatory compliance. Often times, members of an organization are asked for their predicted expenses in a category such as hiring expenses. Not knowing the exact amount of money that will be needed forces many individuals to "pad" the budget so that once it gets reduced by management, there will still be sufficient funds for all the expenses. This is referred to as budget slack. This padding or cushion is an allowance for contingencies that are built into the budget.

Basic Budgeting Definitions

Zero-based Budgeting makes managers prioritize the activities that are carried out in their departments while also justifying their expenditures for each budget period.

Rolling Budget is prepared for several periods in the future, then revised several times prior to the budget period.

Single-period Budget is prepared only once prior to the budget period.

Continuous Budgets can be more expensive to maintain than single-period budgets because more time and effort is required in their preparation.

Average Costs are not that meaningful since all costs are lumped together and then divided by some measure such as quantity of output.

Marginal Costs although challenging to understand, this is a meaningful financial measure. The term marginal means the last. So the marginal cost is the cost from the last unit produced, and marginal revenue means revenue not overall or average but just from the last unit sold.

Standards are most suitably used to support the planning and control processes of the firm. Standards are likely to be most useful when expressed in terms easily related to by the individual whose performance is being evaluated.

Inventory Categories, Carrying Costs, and Economic Order Quantity

Budgets for manufacturing companies are affected by the amounts of different categories of inventory. Budgets are based on reasonable assumptions and expectations of both costs and future sales. (We discuss the sales aspect below but start with the cost or inventory aspect first.) For a manufacturing company, some of the costs include the inventory, which is either ready for sale or in various stages of the manufacturing process.

Inventory for manufacturing companies is usually listed on the balance sheet under one of the following three categories: materials, work-in-process, or finished goods. There are costs involved with either running out of salable inventory (called a stock out) or having too much inventory. The cost of having too much inventory includes carrying costs that include interest on funds invested in building up inventory levels, warehousing costs, and handling expenses.

One formula that finance managers sometimes use to calculate the optimal level of inventory is the economic order quantity (EOQ). EOQ requires knowing the total sales in units, the ordering cost for each order, and the carrying cost per unit. The actual calculation of EOQ is beyond the scope of this book, so we are simply introducing the topic so that the HR professional understands that it relates to inventory levels.

The Sales/Revenue Forecast

As mentioned above, budgets are based on reasonable expectations or assumptions about future events. Budgets are usually based on expectations of the level of sales that can be obtained by the company.

Human resources can be instrumental in developing the sales forecast, which will be the foundation for all the other important budgets for the organization. Human resources can be involved in a couple of ways. For example, human resources often hires and works with the company's sales force leadership with training and management of the employees obtaining the company's sales goals. By keeping the lines of communication open, human resources can gain some important information about the trends and challenges that the sales force is experiencing. Realistically, the main avenue in which human resources would know about the sales trends would be from management meetings when different functional areas of the company meet.

Cash Budget

In the cash budget, the components include the anticipated collections of accounts receivable on a monthly basis. Cash budgets include series of cash receipts, disbursements, and the resulting borrowing requirements if and when there is a shortfall in funds. It is derived from the pro forma income statement and other supporting schedules. Pro forma means projected. For example, the company could expect to receive 50 percent of its current month's sales immediately in the form of cash. It may not receive the other 50 percent until one or two months have passed. This could be 30 percent in month two after the sale and the last 20 percent in month three after the sale. Even though the other 50 percent of this current month's sales may not be received in full for another two months, keep in mind that previous months' sales are being collected this month using the same pattern of collection. That means that part of this month's sales and part of last month's sales are being received by the company.

This is especially important for the organization to know since it may be forced into a position of having to negotiate a short-term bank loan.

Here is an example of a partial cash budget. This is the top portion of the cash budget that shows the timeframe in which the sales are collected in the form of cash.

Partial Cash Budget

	April	May	June	July	August
Sales	$540,000	$396,000	$480,000	$240,000	$408,000
Cash Sales 20%	108,000	79,200	96,000	48,000	81,600
Credit Sales 80%	432,000	316,800	384,000	192,000	326,400
Collections (lagged 1 month-30%)		129,600	95,040	115,200	57,600
Collections (lagged 2 months-70%)			302,400	221,760	268,800
Total Cash Receipts			**$1,357,440**	**$816,960**	**$1,142,400**

Here is an example of a basic but complete cash budget. We will use the same numbers calculated above. Notice that the cash receipts per month are the starting place for the complete cash budget.

Cash Budget

	June	July	August
Total Cash Receipts	$1,357,440	$816,960	$1,142,400
Total Cash Payments	(987,000)	(967,000)	(2,220,500)
Net Cash Flow	$370,440	$(150,040)	($1,078,100)
Beginning Cash Balance	$700,000*	$1,070,400	$920,400
Ending Cash Balance	$1,070,440	$920,400	$ (157,700)

*Beginning Cash for June was Ending Cash from the end of month May.
(Remember that ( ) brackets mean a negative number or subtraction. Minus signs are not used in accounting.)

This is a fairly basic cash budget since there are no loans being paid. The bottom line is that in June the organization's cash flow is the best of the three months. The cash receipts exceeded the cash payments, which increased the cash balance. This ending cash balance in June was the beginning cash balance for July.

In July, the cash payments exceeded the cash receipts, which then decreased the cumulative, or running, cash balance. The ending cash was still a positive number of $920,360, so no loans had to be taken out to cover expenses in the short run. However, in August, the cash payments far surpassed cash receipts, and there was not enough cash in the account to cover the need for cash in August. A negative cash balance resulted. This may have to be covered with a short-term loan.

Sales Budget

The sales budget is an estimate of future sales, often broken down into both units and dollars. It is used to create company sales goals.

The following are important factors to consider when preparing a sales forecast: the state of the economy, seasonal demand variations, and competitors' actions. Human resources would be most likely involved in providing information for creation of the sales budget based on the level of staffing in both operations and the sales force. For example, insufficient numbers of employees in the operations of the company could lead to slow growth in sales volume.

Next is an example of a basic sales budget.

Budgeted sales in units	45,000	33,000	40,000	20,000	34,000
Selling price per unit	x $12	x $12	x $12	x $12	x $12
Total sales	$540,000	$396,000	$480,000	$240,000	$408,000

Total sales are calculated by multiplying sales units by the selling price per unit.

Production Budget

Product-oriented companies create a production budget. It is an estimate of the number of units that must be manufactured in order to meet the sales goals. The production budget also estimates the various costs involved with manufacturing those units, such as labor, material, and other expenses.

The production budget uses all of the following except the cash receipts budget.

Production Schedule

	April	May	June	July
Forecasted unit sales	4,000	10,000	8,000	6,000
+Desired ending inventory	15,000	12,000	9,000	
−Beginning inventory	6,000	15,000	12,000	
Units to be produced	13,000	7,000	5,000	
Cash Payments	**Feb**	**March**	**April**	**May**
Units produced	8,000	13,000	7,000	5,000
Materials ($7/unit) month after production		$56,000	$91,000	$49,000
Labor ($3/unit) month of production		39,000	21,000	15,000
Fixed overhead		10,000	10,000	10,000
Dividends				14,000
Total Cash Payments		$105,000	$122,000	$88,000

Additional Budgets

A materials purchases budget must be completed immediately after the preparation of the production budget.

An inventory purchases budget would be used for companies that purchase rather than produce their inventory which will be sold later at a higher price than it was purchased for.

Inventory Purchases Budget

	June	July	August
Budgeted cost of goods sold	$70,000	$80,000	$86,000
Plus desired ending inventory	8,000	7,600	9,000
Inventory needed	78,000	87,600	95,000
Less beginning inventory	10,000	8,000	8,600
Required purchases (on account)	68,000	79,600	86,400

The marketing budget is an estimate of the funds needed for promotion, advertising, and public relations in order to market the product or service.

The project budget is a prediction of the costs associated with a particular company project. These costs include labor, materials, and other related expenses. This budget is often broken down into specific tasks, with task budgets assigned to each.

Cost Analysis for Decision Making

Management typically makes decisions with numerous implicit constraints, a few of which are discussed here. The concepts discussed below are part of the conceptual framework in which management operates. The following concepts of the time value of money, opportunity cost, and sunk costs are fundamental in many business decisions. When HR professionals are familiar with these terms, they can then understand them in the context of their organization. This puts them at a distinct advantage over other less informed HR professionals. The concepts that follow are often the basis for both developing and implementing business strategy. Their usefulness cannot be over-emphasized.

Implicit Constraint of Time Value of Money

The time value of money is a concept that is related to the value of money increasing over time. The two components are present value and future value. Inflation is ignored. The two variables include the interest rate per period and the number of periods, usually stated in years. The future value of money is always larger than the present value of money.

The present value of money is the value of money in today's terms. Money grows from accrual of interest over time. For example, $1.00 today does not have the same value as $1.00 in 10 years. Ignoring inflation, would you consider loaning someone some money and receiving the same amount, vs. a larger amount if the loan was for 10 or 20 years?

This relates to the next topic of capital budgeting since this type of budgeting is for the long term. Examples of capital budgeting include monies set aside today at a certain interest rate for a project such as a new building to be built 15 years hence. How would the finance director know how much to invest today if the number of years and interest rate were not known? Therefore, time value of money is important.

To calculate the time value of money, you need to know three of the following pieces of information:

- the interest rate per period
- the number of periods (normally stated in terms of years)
- the present value (PV)
- the future value (FV)

Human resources must recognize that there are numerous examples of how present value and future value decisions made in their organization affect them. For example, if there is a costly strategic initiative—such as a long-term training program—the organization may put funds aside for the program to start several years later. Human resources would be aware that money grows over time and that the interest rate directly affects that growth. During years of low interest rates, more money must be invested or put aside to have enough for the HR program in the future.

Calculating Present Value and Future Value

There are three ways to calculate present value and future value. They include using a formula, using a financial calculator, and using present value and future value tables. We will be referring to the most common approach, which is using the tables. The examples shown below will be calculated using the values from either a PV or a FV table. The tables are not shown since the actual calculations are beyond the scope of this book.

Capital Budgeting and HR

Capital budgeting can be considered a subset of budgeting for a couple of reasons. First, capital budgeting focuses on ways to measure the viability of investing in certain projects in the future. Budgets in general focus on the near future, whereas capital budgeting is always long-term in nature.

The capital budget is a prediction of company needs in regard to *fixed assets*, such as buildings, vehicles, machinery, and other equipment. For example, suppose that Lands' End, the merchandising company, purchases a new computer system to enhance its customer billing system or Ford Motor Company purchases a new plant in another country and needs extensive levels of machinery and equipment.

There are three widely accepted methods of evaluating capital expenditures:

- The payback method
- The net present value method, and
- The internal rate of return (IRR) method.

Each one will be explained, and then an example will be shown.

We will start with the most basic or simple way to analyze a capital budgeting expenditure to see if it is a good, viable option for the organization.

The Payback Method

The payback method is a method that analyzes how quickly extra money comes into the organization as a result of the investment, compared to the initial cost of the investment. Basically, if money is invested today and cash is spent, how quickly will this investment result in cash coming into the organization? Assume a $100,000 investment and the following cash inflows for two scenarios. What we are analyzing is when the $100,000 investment will be recovered or paid back. In this example two possible investments are being compared to each other.

Year	Investment K	Investment M
1	$30,000	$40,000
2	50,000	30,000
3	20,000	15,000
4	60,000	15,000
5	—	50,000

Which of the two alternatives would you select under the payback method?

Analysis:

Payback for Investment K		Payback for Investment M	
$100,000–$30,000	1 year	$100,000–40,000	1 year
70,000– 50,000	2 years	60,000–30,000	2 years
20,000– 20,000	3 years	30,000–15,000	3 years
		15,000–15,000	4 years

Payback Investment K = 3 years

Payback Investment M= 4 years

Investment K should be selected because of the faster payback.

Net Present Value Method

Another way to use to analyze the viability of a capital project is the net present value method. Using this method requires a strong understanding of the time value of money concept. As a reminder, time value of money is a key business concept for management in all functional areas. We will be using the most common way to calculate the present value and the future value by using tables to obtain the interest factors. Interest factors are simply a singular number that is looked up in the appropriate table based on the two variables of N (number of years normally) and I (the interest rate). In this example, I have already looked up the interest factor and then multiplied by the number that is known. So, if PV (present value) is already known and we are calculating FV (future value), then we will multiply PV by the interest factor we just looked up in the table.

Example of Net Present Value Method

Beta Dynamics will invest $100,000 in a project that will produce the following cash flows. The cost of capital is 11 percent. This means that the interest rate is 11 percent. The issue is whether Beta should undertake this project.

(Note that the fourth year's cash flow is negative.)

Year	Cash Flow
1	$33,000
2	40,000
3	32,000
4	(44,000)
5	61,000

What we are focusing on is finding the present value of these future cash flows. We are trying to find out what these future cash flows are worth *now*, in present value terms. In the table below you will see that there are five years of cash inflows, money coming into the organization as a result of the investment of $100,000 into this capital project. We assume an interest rate of 11 percent and find the PV factor (from a table or financial calculator) for each year. We are multiplying the cash inflow each year by the PV factor, then adding all five years' results to get our answer.

Beta Dynamics

Year	Cash Flow	PV$_{IF}$ at 11%	Present Value
1	$33,000	.901	$ 29,733
2	40,000	.812	32,480
3	32,000	.731	23,392
4	(44,000)	.659	(28,996)
5	61,000	.593	36,173
	Total		$92,782

In this example we see that the PV of all these future cash inflows to the organization are worth $92,782 in today's dollars. Granted, this interest rate is very high and that is not always relevant, but we now need to compare this total to our $100,000 investment. Since the outflow of $100,000 exceeds the present value of the inflows, we should *not* invest in this capital expenditure since the financial rewards are less than the $100,000 investment.

Internal Rate of Return

The last method we will discuss, the internal rate of return (IRR), is the most accurate and accepted way to analyze capital expenditures. Be forewarned, however, it is also very complex.

"The IRR method requires calculation of the rate that equates the cash investment with the cash inflows." IRR is a tool to

> "measure and compare the profitability of investments. It is an indicator of the efficiency, quality, or yield of an investment as compared to the net present value tool, which is an indicator of the value or magnitude of an investment."[1]

Calculating the IRR is an aspect of capital budgeting because a decision has to be made about the usefulness of making this capital expenditure. Does it make sense to spend the money now to have cash inflow as a result of this project?

ABC Company uses the IRR process of capital rationing in its decision making. The firm's cost of capital is 12 percent. The investment is $85,000 this year. It has determined the internal rate of return for each of the following projects.

Project	Project Size	Percent of Internal Rate of Return
R	$35,000	14%
S	32,000	19
T	10,000	10
U	45,000	16.5
V	10,000	21
W	12,000	11
X	25,000	18
Y	14,000	17.5

Rank the Investments in Terms of IRR

Project	IRR	Project Size	Total Budget
V	21	$10,000	$10,000
S	19	$32,000	$42,000
X	18	$25,000	$67,000
Y	17.5	$14,000	$81,000

The projects should be chosen based on the internal rate of return that is in excess of the cost of capital of 12 percent and the total of which does not exceed the money available. In this case, the company had $85,000 to spend.

Flexible Budgets vs. Static Budgets

Before we introduce an example of a flexible budget, let's define some terms that relate directly to this type of budget. Variable costs are expenses that vary up or down depending on the level of output. Example: flour used for pizzas ordered at a pizzeria.

Fixed costs are expenses that occur and have to be paid regardless of the level of output. Examples include the CEO's salary and the cost of the building. Even though this concept of fixed costs is very important, there is no way to trace these numbers directly to the financial statements. The cost accountants for the organization would have the calculations on worksheets.

A flexible budget is prepared to compare actual results to the budgeted numbers. These budgets are based on more than one level of activity. The column on the far right of the report shows the actual and budgeted amounts and the differences, or variances, between these amounts. Each variance is analyzed separately and may be favorable or unfavorable. An example will be shown below.

Total budget variance is caused by the factors of quantity and price.

On the other hand, static budgets only show one level of activity. They work best when you are evaluating performance and the planned level of activity is the *same* as the actual level of activity.

As first defined above, flexible budgets are based on more than one level of activity. They are more realistic since they are calculated based on two different levels of units produced. As you will see in the example below, there is an original budget based on 35,000 units being produced. A unit could be pizzas in a pizza shop or haircuts at a beauty salon. This is compared to 33,250 units produced in actuality. Each expense is then analyzed as either favorable (less is spent than anticipated) or unfavorable (more is spent than anticipated). In this example unfavorable variances are denoted with a "U" and favorable variances are denoted with an "F." Budget variance is the total variance for any particular cost component.

Item	Original Budget (35,000 units)	Flexed Budget (33,250 units)	Actual Cost	Variance	
Direct Materials	$498,050	$473,148	$498,000	($24,852)	U
Direct Labor	385,000	365,750	413,500	($47,750)	U
Variable Overhead	218,750	207,813	195,250	$12,563	F
Fixed Overhead	148,050	140,648	172,500	($31,852)	U
Total	$1,249,850	$1,187,358	$1,279,250	($91,893)	U

For each expense category, the flexed budget is compared to the actual costs. In all expenses in this example, except the allocation of variable overhead, the variances have been unfavorable. This is shown as a "U" on the budget.

Static budgets are just that: static, unchanging. They are less realistic and less useful than flexible budgets because they do not use more than one level of activity. Yet, static budgets are often used since they are easier to create and interpret.

Relevant Costs and Avoidable Costs

Incremental analysis is the method of evaluating financial data that change under different courses of action. So, instead of analyzing all aspects of a project or decision, incremental analysis focuses on just one part of the project or process. Relevant costs are costs that can change a decision. For example, if the company is deciding which health benefits plan to choose for its employees and the deductible for many procedures is too costly, this is a relevant cost since it is significant enough to make a difference in the decision related to this health benefits package. So, if Company A's health plan costs are significantly higher than what Company B is offering, the company must decide whether or not the cost difference is significant. There is no blanket rule for all companies purchasing something such as health benefits for its employees. If health benefits, for example, have risen about 3 percent per year using Company B's plan, then Company B suddenly raises them by 5 percent, this added expense may be considered relevant because the excessive costs will trigger a different decision (i.e., choosing Company A instead).

Avoidable costs. If the company chooses to make or buy a component of its product, there are some costs that would not exist for each of the two decisions. They include the variable costs of direct materials and direct labor if the organization needs to train its 500 employees on its new diversity initiative. The organization can use internal human resources and legal staff to conduct the training, it can bring in outside trainers, or it can send employees to various local training programs.

Human resources can play a significant role in making decisions for the organization based on relevant costs. In this example, Niva Company would consider the following costs as relevant to the decision to enter the medical apparatus market: design and engineering costs, new equipment, raw materials, direct labor, variable overhead, any possible new fixed overhead costs such as a production supervisor that may be dedicated to this product line. It is important to note that no new facility costs are required for this product line since the current manufacturing plant has sufficient square footage to accommodate the new product line. For hiring purposes, human resources would have to know and understand the decision about relevant costs and the make or buy question.

In this example we define relevant costs to make the part internally as those costs that would be avoided if the part were continued to be purchased from the outside. Avoidable costs would include direct material, direct labor, variable overhead, and the new manager's salary.

Here we do a side-by-side analysis to see which is less expensive for the company: to make (internal production) or buy from another company.

	Estimated Production Costs	Avoidable Cost if Purchased
Manufacturing costs:		
Direct material	$ 28	$ 28
Direct labor	8	8
Variable overhead	4	4
Fixed overhead	7	3
Total cost per unit	$ 47	$ 43
Purchase costs if purchased from another company:		
Outside purchase cost		$ 39
Shipping and other costs		4
Total purchase cost		$ 43

From a quantitative standpoint, Niva Company is indifferent about the decision. The cost to buy is the same as the avoidable costs if purchased. However, there are other concerns or factors that could influence Niva Company on whether it makes or buys this part. These factors might include the following:

- The potential for improved control over the availability of the parts by having them as needed;
- The potential for improved quality of the parts; and
- Best use of currently available capacity (are there any relevant opportunity costs of using this capacity for more profitable activities?).

HR and the Make or Buy Question

This fundamental decision about whether to produce or purchase components in a manufacturing company relates directly to budgeting because the ultimate cost of these items will become a component of the budget. Manufacturing companies often outsource part of the process in order to keep costs down.

If an organization chooses to make a component of the product it sells, human resources must be aware that more employees will be involved in the manufacturing of this component. If human resources is also involved in negotiations with outside vendors, then human resources may be involved in contacting and negotiating price and quantity discounts with these individuals.

The price of either making or buying components is the driving force. Intuitively it might seem that it is always better to make rather than buy components, but that is often not the case. Perhaps the organization does not have sufficient space to produce this component or the number of employees is not high enough to support this part of the manufacturing process.

Not Staying Within the Budget

Overspending in one department can have a ripple effect throughout the organization. If the organization's bottom line, net income, turns into net loss, this loss must be made up from other sources. When any organizational department exceeds its budget, there will be fewer financial resources for other departments. Human resources is affected when others within the organization do not stay within budget because there is less money available for hiring and training and some compensation levels may be lowered. In addition, the company may be looking for new hires who are willing and able to start at lower salaries and laying off seasoned, higher-paid employees. For a sole proprietorship, the loss comes out of the single owner's capital account. For corporations, retained earnings will decrease in the short run.

Why Retained Earnings Matter

Retained earnings are the current and previous organizational level earnings that are kept in the organization in order for it to grow or expand. Organizations that continually suffer from net losses will have less chance to maintain their competitive advantage. When organizations do not stay within their self-imposed budgets, the bottom line (net income) is affected. Retained earnings, which represent current and previous years' net income, are kept in the organization rather than distributed to shareholders in the form of cash dividends. Budgets must be adhered to in order for the organization to minimize its expenses, which affects net income and ultimately retained earnings.

All organizations are either growing or contracting. HR professionals can play a viable role in helping their organization to keep growing. When human resources and hiring managers hire the right people for critical roles within the organization, there is more likelihood that better decisions will be made and more innovations may occur. Human resources also plays an important role in monitoring the performance of all employees and making appropriate training opportunities available.

Who decides if the organization may not still be in business within the near future? Auditors. This concept of going concern (which means whether or not the company may exist in the near future) is critical for shareholders to know.

Strong Correlation Between Budgeting and Business Literacy Competency

Budgeting is often considered to be one of the more complex business literacy concepts. Therefore, the level of financial knowledge required to fully understand the budgeting process in its entirety requires a stronger base. For example, one of the last steps in the budget creation process is creation of the pro forma balance sheet and the pro forma income statement. The latter is an estimate of future income, which is based on educated guesses about future revenue and expenses. Valid assumptions must be made in order to create pro forma statements.

Example: Leena Corporation: Pro Forma Income Statement

	Sept.	Oct.	Nov.	Total
Sales	$245,900	$197,000	$245,000	$687,900
Cost of Goods Sold	$(126,700)	$(98,400)	$(123,000)	$(348,100)
Gross Profit	$119,200	$98,600	$122,000	$339,800
Selling and Administrative Expense	$42,400	$37,200	$43,400	$123,000
Interest Expense	$3,200	$3,200	$3,200	$9,600
Net Profit Before Tax	$73,600	$58,200	$75,400	$207,200
Taxes	$27,493	$21,534	$27,898	$76,925
Net Profit After Tax	$46,107	$36,666	$47,502	$130,275
Less: Common Dividends				$(24,000)
Increase in Retained Earnings				$106,275

Cash Flow Planning as an Integral Part of Forecasting

As mentioned above, making good decisions regarding cash can mean the difference between the organization failing and the organization thriving. Forecasting involves makes predictions or educated guesses about the future based on assumptions. For many organizations, anticipating or forecasting cash flow inflows and outflows is critical to financial survival.

The chief financial officer (CFO) or organizational equivalent makes daily decisions about how to obtain and use funding for the organization. Human resources hired the CFO and most likely works with this finance department to keep employees engaged and well-trained. Cash is the lifeblood of an organization, and managing it can be enormously complex.

Forecasting is based on assumptions about possible future events and from past events or trends.

Companies will vary tremendously on how they obtain and use cash. Here are some examples of major sources and uses of cash.

Sources

- Operating cash flows (sales of the company's products and services)
- Short-term borrowings
- Long-term borrowings
- Asset or business sales

Uses

- Asset purchases
- Dividends distributed to shareholders
- Repayment of short-term debt
- Repayment of long-term debt
- Business acquisition

What You Should Know

- Budgeting is challenging since many assumptions must be made.
- There are many types of budgets, and organizations need to decide which ones are necessary and work best for them.
- Forecasted sales are the starting place for many other budgets.
- Pro forma means projected.
- Time value of money analyzes present value vs. future value of money. You must know the interest rate, number of periods, and either present value or future value to do a calculation.

- Capital budgeting equates to long-term planning for items such as property, plant, and equipment.
- There are three accepted methods of analyzing the cost-effectiveness of capital budgeting projects: payback method, net present value method, and internal rate of return (IRR).
- IRR is typically the best way to analyze whether or not to invest in a capital project.
- Flexible budgets are created if the actual level of activity is different from the budgeted level. They are more useful and show current instead of proposed levels of production activity. A variance is the difference between actual costs and expected costs.

CHAPTER 9

Financial Ratios

Financial ratios are a powerful tool to assess various relationships between the numbers from the financial statements. They are derived from the financial statements and used in conjunction with financial statement analysis. Financial ratios are often calculated by managers and by auditors because looking at the financial statements alone will *not* tell the entire story behind the numbers.

One kind of financial ratio, for instance, is the relationship between current assets and current liabilities. By way of example, suppose Preeta Printers has current assets of $120,000 and current liabilities of $60,000. The ratio is to divide liabilities into assets (A/L) for an answer of 2. For each dollar in current liabilities (the denominator) there is twice as much money in current assets. It is a good thing having more current assets than current liabilities. Most organizations strive to have a current ratio of at least 1, which means that for every $1 in liabilities there is $1 in assets.

Nonprofits and for-profit organizations do not differ in their goal of having a higher current ratio. This ratio is not directly tied to the level of profitability. Instead, this ratio indicates the organization's ability to pay its current or short-term debts.

Key Financial Ratios and Examples

The following ratios help determine whether the company is running its business well and how profitable the company is compared to its competitors.

Gross Profit Margin

Gross profit margin equals sales minus the cost of goods sold divided by sales. What does it tell you? The amount of sales that a company keeps in the form of gross profit. It is usually given as a percentage. It is a key performance measure (HR professionals, do not confuse this with employee performance measurements).

	ABC Company	NYW Company
Sales	$10,325,000	$2,090,000
COGS	$7,844,000	$1,400,900
(Sales-COGS)/Sales	24.03%	32.97%

In this scenario, NYW's gross margin is better. As a proportion of sales (although lower than ABC Company), it kept its cost of goods sold (COGS) lower. Controlling costs (i.e., COGS) is critical.

Operating Margin

The operating margin is equal to the operating income divided by sales. What does it tell you? What a company makes or loses from its primary business on each dollar of sales.

	ABC Company	NYW Company
Operating Income	$897,000	$312,000
Sales	$10,325,000	$2,090,000
Operating Income/Sales	8.69%	14.93%

NYW is in better shape regarding the operating margin. It has a higher operating income as a percentage of sales.

Liquidity Ratios

These ratios answer the question of the ability of the organization to pay its short-term financial obligations.

Current Ratio

Current ratio is equal to current assets divided by current liabilities What does it tell you? This is the most basic liquidity test, and it signifies whether or not the organization can pay its obligations.

	ABC Company	NYW Company
Current Assets	$3,090,080	$2,472,064
Current Liabilities	$2,354,000	$2,118,600
Current Assets ÷ Current Liabilities	1.31	1.17

For this ratio, ABC Company is slightly stronger and its liquidity, or ability to pay its short-term obligations, is better than NYW Company's.

Quick Ratio

Quick ratio is equal to cash plus accounts receivable plus short-term (or marketable) securities divided by current liabilities. What does it tell you? It is a tougher test of liquidity. Like the current ratio, the higher the number the more liquid the company is and thus better equipped to weather economic challenges.

Working Capital Ratio

Working capital ratio is equal to current assets minus current liabilities. What does it tell you? It is simply the difference between current assets and current liabilities. It is a key metric for measuring liquidity, the organization's ability to pay its short-term financial obligations. Example: payroll. The larger the number, the better the position of the company. Here ABC Company is better since the number is higher.

	ABC Company	NYW Company
Current Assets	$3,090,080	$2,472,064
Current Liabilities	$2,354,000	$2,118,600
Current Assets − Current Liabilities	$736,080	$353,464

Collection Period

The collection period is equal to the average accounts receivable multiplied by 360 and then divided by sales. What does it tell you? Minimizing the number of days in which customers pay the business for services already rendered is critical in maintaining adequate cash flow. Small numbers are better.

Leverage Ratios (Capital Structure)

These ratios measure the amount of debt that exists on the balance sheet. Implicitly the more debt, the riskier it is for shareholders since debt holders have first claim against the organization's assets.

Debt/Equity. Debt/Equity equals short-term debt plus long-term debt divided by total equity. What does it tell you? It tells you how much of the company is financed by debt versus its owners (shareholders). Lower ratios can indicate less risk, everything else being held constant.

	ABC Company	NYW Company
Total liabilities	$4,943,400	$4,872,780
Total equity	$9,033,459	$10,840,151
Debt-to-equity ratio	0.55	0.45

ABC Company has a riskier capital structure than does NYW Company. Again, for this particular ratio, smaller numbers are better.

Total Debt Ratio. Total debt ratio is equal to total liabilities divided by total assets. What does it tell you? This ratio shows you the level or percentage of assets that are financed through debt. Lower numbers are often considered better because too much debt is risky for an organization.

	ABC Company	NYW Company
Total liabilities	$4,943,400	$4,872,780
Total assets	$13,976,859	$15,712,931
Total debt ratio	0.35	0.31

NYW is in better shape for this ratio since it has fewer liabilities per its level of total assets.

Operational/Efficiency Ratios

Efficiency ratios measure the following areas within an organization: the quality of a business' receivables, how well it uses and controls its assets, how effectively the organization is paying suppliers, and whether the organization is using borrowed funds. Efficiency ratios can reflect how well an organization plans and controls financing and use of its assets.

Inventory Turnover

Inventory turnover equals cost of goods sold (COGS) divided by average inventory. What does it tell you? It tells you how well an organization manages its inventory levels. Overstocking or running out of inventory are both bad situations. All else being equal, higher inventory turnover is better.

	ABC Company	NYW Company
COGS	$7,844,000	$1,400,900
Average Inventory	$2,300,000	$546,000
Inventory Turnover	3.41	2.57

ABC Company is doing a better job selling its inventory instead of storing it for future sale. Companies need to continually sell their inventory in a quick and efficient manner.

Accounts Receivable Turnover

Accounts receivable turnover is equal to revenue divided by the average accounts receivable. What does it tell you? It tells you how quickly or efficiently the organization is billing its customers from sales volume and how well the organization is collecting from its customers.

	ABC Company	NYW Company
Revenue	$10,325,000	$2,090,000
Average Accounts Receivable	$1,090,000	$342,900
Accounts Receivable Turnover ratio	9.47	6.10

ABC is much better at collecting the money owed to it by its customers from prior sales. Larger numbers are better.

Accounts Payable Turnover

Accounts payable turnover is equal to cost of goods sold (COGS) divided by the average accounts payable. What does it tell you? It measures the rate at which an organization pays its suppliers.

	ABC Company	NYW Company
COGS	$7,844,000	$1,400,900
Average Accounts Payable	$768,000	$564,000
COGS/Average Accounts Payable	10.21	2.48

ABC Company is much faster and better at paying its suppliers. This is good as long as the company does not pay them too quickly and miss out on earning interest on the money it owes the suppliers.

Earnings per Share

Earnings per share (EPS) is a critical financial ratio. It is one of several indications of the financial strength of an organization. Shareholders are very interested in this number because it indicates their part of the earnings after taxes. EPS is equal to earnings after taxes minus preferred dividends divided by the weighted average of shares outstanding. What does it tell you? The amount of net income that is left to distribute to common shareholders after deducting any preferred dividends (if applicable).

In this simple example, we will show how this number is calculated:

Brown Paper Company had earnings after taxes of $580,000 last year with 400,000 weighted average of shares of stock outstanding.

Earnings per share = Earnings after taxes/Weighted average of Shares outstanding

or

EPS = $580,000/400,000 = $1.45

As mentioned above, earnings per share is equal to the after tax earnings minus preferred stock dividends (if applicable) divided by the weighted average of common shares outstanding. What this means is that each common stock share is "assigned" part of the net income that is left over after the preferred shareholders have been paid. So, when human resources hires the right people for the right jobs and keeps their own department level expenses to a minimum, human resources is adding to the bottom line. The higher the bottom line/net income, the higher the earnings per share. In other words, shareholders have a significant vested interest in the level of EPS.

Diluted Earnings per Share

Basic earnings per share do not consider the potentially dilutive effects of convertibles, warrants, and other securities that can generate new shares of common stock. (Convertibles are investments that can be changed into shares of stock.) If and when this happens, the earnings are spread out or diluted over more shares of stock. That means each shareholder receives less earnings for every share owned.

Price-Earnings Ratio

Price-earnings ratio (P/E ratio) is a favored metric of what the market will pay for a share of stock. It is calculated by dividing price into earnings per share. The higher the number, the higher the price investors *may be* willing to pay for a share of stock. Higher numbers can also mean that the stock is overpriced.

The factors that might affect or influence the P/E ratio could include the earnings and sales growth and potential growth of the company, investors' perceptions, the level of risk or how volatile the earnings are, the debt and equity structure, and numerous other factors. Investors often track P/E ratios and make many assumptions about the future of that company and its stock price based on this ratio.

Break-Even Analysis

Break-even analysis is critical to new companies and those that are making strategic decisions about adding or deleting a product line. Break-even analysis is fairly fluid, meaning that a change in one or more variables will affect the company's ability to break even. For example, if the selling price increases for a product or service, the company will break even sooner. Another example could involve a change in the variable costs such as labor costs. When labor costs increase, it takes longer for the company to break even. Break-even analysis applies to service-oriented companies also. Fundamentally, the break-even point is when there is neither a profit nor a loss. It can be described in either the level of break-even units sold or the break-even revenue dollars.

Example: ABC Appliance

ABC Appliance mixers sell for $20 per unit, and the variable cost to produce them is $15. First, the company estimates that the fixed costs are $80,000. How is the break-even point in units calculated? Secondly, fill in the table below.

Sales	_____
– Fixed costs	_____
– Total variable costs	_____
Net profit (loss)	_____

Break-even is calculated as follows: BE = Fixed costs/Price-variable cost per unit

BE = $80,000/$20-$15 = $80,000/$5 = 16,000 units

Answer to part two of the question:

Sales	$320,000 (16,000 units × $20)
–Fixed costs	$ 80,000
–Total variable costs	<u>240,000</u> (16,000 units × $15)
Net profit (loss)	$ 0

The Break-Even Ratio and HR

If an organization's sales are too low or its variable costs (such as labor costs) are too high, then the organization is at risk for short-term liquidity and/or long-term solvency issues. Liquidity is the ease with which assets are turned into cash. Liquidity is important for organizations since it represents their ability to pay their short-term financial obligations in a timely fashion. Solvency is the long-term equivalent in that it represents an organization's ability to pay its long-term financial obligations. Companies must cover both their variable and fixed costs from sales. Once these two types of costs are covered, sales will yield the organization some profit. For most organizations, knowing the price and volume it takes to cover these expenses is important since companies are in business to make money (unless they are nonprofits, of course).

This is important to human resources because both fixed costs (such as equipment and buildings) and variable costs (such as labor costs) must be kept to a minimum. Once all costs are covered, the company can start realizing or attaining profitability. The concept of break-even is critical for start-up companies and for companies with high fixed costs. Human resources plays an important role here by making sure the company doesn't overcompensate for talent, by negotiating the reduction in cost of benefits, etc.

Return on Investment and Return on Equity

Return on investment (ROI) and return on equity (ROE) are both important ratios, but when they are used together they give management a much broader, comprehensive view of the organization.

ROI

As a reminder, ROI deals with measuring an organization's profitability and is calculated by dividing income into assets. The larger the number the better. It is represented by the following formula: net income/assets. In financial terms, successful companies maximize net income (the numerator in the ROI formula) while minimizing the use of company assets such as equipment. This means getting the most out of what you invest in assets in the company.

ROI is equal to the net income divided by average assets. In accounting, the price or cost of assets does not change on the balance sheet. Assets are recorded at their original cost. Larger numbers are better.

ROE

ROE "measures a corporation's profitability by revealing how much profit a company generates with the money shareholders have invested."[1] There are two ways of calculating ROE: the traditional formula and the DuPont formula. The traditional approach divides the company's net profit after taxes for the past 12 months by stockholders' equity (adjusted for stock splits). But this fails to account for the effect of borrowed funds, which can magnify the returns posted by even a poorly managed company. An alternative approach, developed by the DuPont Corporation, links ROE to financial leverage (use of debt).

Traditional Formula:

ROE = Net Profit After Taxes ÷ Stockholders' Equity

DuPont Formula:

ROE = ROI x Equity Multiplier

ROE = (Net Profit After Taxes ÷ Total Assets) x (Total Assets ÷ Stockholders' Equity)

For example, using the traditional formula, a company with $18,000 in net profit after taxes and $45,000 in stockholders' equity would have an ROE of 40 percent. The DuPont formula takes the analysis one step further by factoring in the contribution of borrowed funds. Using the previous example, if the company has total assets of $100,000, then $55,000 of the company's capital is supplied by creditors and its equity multiplier is 2.22.

ROE = ($18,000 ÷ $100,000) x ($100,000 ÷ $45,000)

ROE = 18% x 2.22

ROE = 40%

Note: If the company did not use any borrowed funds, its equity multiplier would be 1.0 and its ROE would equal its ROI.[2]

ROE is equal to the net income divided by the average owners' equity. Larger numbers are better and mean that more income is generated with less owner investment.

Shareholders' investments need to be used as efficiently and effectively as possible to maximize the company's net income. As seen below, these two ratios are interrelated.

ROI	=	Margin	x	Turnover	ROE
Net Income Average Assets	=	Net Income Sales	×	Sales Average Assets	Net Income Average Owners' Equity

Risk

The role of risk in organizational decisions ratios is often scrutinized by investors, auditors, and management since ratios tell a story about the interrelationships between the financial aspects of an organization. For example, the profit margin indicates how much net income is left over from sales revenue. Different individuals view the financial ratios from their own perspectives. Not all of these individuals within and outside of an organization have the same level of risk tolerance. Some ratio results indicate potential risky behavior on the part of management.

Shareholders (and owners in general) and management tend to view risk differently. Risk is often a component of business decisions. Not all individuals are risk adverse, meaning they do not shy away from risk. One extreme example of a company that thrived on high levels of risk and made risky decisions on a regular basis was Enron. For years this strategy of thinking outside the box and undertaking risky ventures in hopes of high returns worked well for Enron. It was only when it took this strategy to extremes that the company imploded.

HR professionals should not make assumptions about their organization's propensity or disposition to make decisions wrought with risk. However, since human resources is a part of an organization's management structure, if they see risky decisions based on, for example, the forecasting of rapid sales growth or rapid expansion without additional hiring and training, then as a member "at the table," human resources is obligated to comment on and question the soundness of these decisions.[3]

Manipulating Ratios

Greedy, desperate, or unethical managers who understand the critical nature of financial ratios can manipulate these ratios to reflect higher returns than actually exist. It almost goes without stating, but financial manipulation isn't just unethical behavior, it is likely grounds for immediate termination and even prosecution. Unfortunately, this situation may not be visible to most managers within the company. Auditors would most likely be the ones who would report any manipulation of the numbers. In the example below, two scenarios are shown. On the left side the company does not prepay its accounts payable (which is more the norm), and on the right side the company does prepay its accounts payable. Notice that if the company prepays its accounts payable, they would be using cash. Cash is a current asset. So, if they prepay their accounts payable, current assets decrease by the same amount that accounts payable, which is a current liability, decreases.

This does not seem to pose an issue at first glance. However, when you compare the current ratio that results from prepaying the accounts payable, you see that the ratio is much higher. Higher current ratios are better since current ratios reflect the company's level of liquidity, which is the ability to pay short-term financial obligations in a timely manner.

	Do Not Prepay Accounts Payable	Pre-pay Accounts Payable
Current assets	$ 12,639	$ 8,789
Current liabilities	(7,480)	(3,630)
Working capital	$ 5,159	$ 5,159
Current ratio	1.69	2.42

Paralleling Ratios to Business Ally

Becoming familiar with both the financial statements and the associated ratios will allow HR professionals to analyze how their organization compares to its competitors. Obtaining industry averages is not difficult. You can go to most public libraries and ask for the RMA analysis book to see how your organization compares to the industry average.[4] Trade and professional associations may also have benchmarking data. Choose your industry, such as oil and gas or manufacturing, and then look up ratios. Your organization may be doing better or worse than its competitors within the same industry.

Finding a specific company's ratios is easy if the company is publicly traded. If that is the case, you can find some ratios on the web. Some good sources for obtaining the annual reports for publicly traded companies can be found on the Securities and Exchange Commission website (www.sec.gov).

Capital Leases vs. Operating Leases

Capital leases and operating leases are discussed in this chapter because how an organization categorizes a lease can affect the results of certain ratios. For example, when a lease is a capital lease, the asset that is being leased is listed on the balance sheet, thereby affecting any ratios that contain total assets.

Capital leases are leases that ultimately transfer ownership of an asset to the renter (lessee). Although the capital lease contract may appear to be a rental agreement, it is actually an agreement in which the renter purchases the asset. Examples of leased assets may include buildings or equipment.

Capital leases result in the renter (lessee) assuming nearly all of the risks and benefits of owning the leased asset. Examples could include automobiles, equipment, or buildings.

A lease is a capital lease if it has *any* of the following characteristics:

- It transfers ownership of the asset to the renter
- It permits the renter to purchase the asset for a small amount of money at the end of the lease
- The lease term is at least 75 percent of the economic life of the asset
- The present value of the lease payments is at least 90 percent of fair value of the asset

Operating leases, by comparison, are what we usually consider a traditional lease wherein the renter never owns the asset that is being rented.

Human resources should be aware of their organization's leasing policies since there are long-term consequences to this seemingly unimportant decision. For example, if the company has only operating leases for its buildings, then the assets (in this case, the buildings) that are owned by the company are minimal. If the owner of the buildings (the lessor) decides to cancel the building lease, the company may have nowhere to operate. This could result in outsourcing, reductions-in-force, downsizing, loss of market share, etc.

What You Should Know

- Interpreting ratios is often more important and valuable than being able to calculate them.
- If you start with incorrect financial numbers the financial ratios will also be wrong.
- Many people, including auditors and management, are interested in seeing financial ratios.

- Ratios are divided into categories.
- Profitability ratios assess a business's ability to generate earnings as compared to its expenses and other relevant costs incurred during a specific period of time.
- Liquidity ratios measure a company's ability to pay off short-term debt. They reflect the company's ability to cover its expenses. The current ratio and the quick ratio are two ratios that provide an indication of the company's liquidity.
- Working Capital—Current assets minus current liabilities. This shows the liquidity level or ability of the organization to pay its short term financial obligations. Manipulation of this ratio can take place and should be recognized.
- Operational Efficiency/Employee Productivity ratios measure the efficiency of employees and corporate resources in earning a profit.
- It's important for both employees of the organization and potential investors to understand EPS and P/E ratios.
- Leverage (capital-structure) ratios reflect the extent to which the company uses debt to finance its operations. The debt ratio and the debt-equity ratio are used for this purpose.
- Break-even analysis is important because variable costs and fixed costs must be covered before any profits can be recognized. When an organization covers all costs with sales dollars, the company has achieved break-even and there is neither a profit nor a loss.
- Financial ratios help everyone understand the interrelationship between two numbers. Analyzing financial ratios helps management of all levels understand trends.
- Financial statement ratios support informed judgments and decision making most effectively when the trend of entity data is compared to the trend of industry data.

CHAPTER 10

Financial Management Issues on the HR Radar

In our fast-paced business environment, being aware of economic trends or legal trends can put you ahead of the curve and increase the value you bring to your organization. So, in this chapter we will provide an overview of some hot topics that are currently affecting, or will soon be affecting, many organizations' strategic decision making and should be on HR's radar.

These topics include internal controls, fraud, waste, and abuse; the Sarbanes-Oxley Act of 2002 and associated whistle-blower hotline; and the International Financial Reporting Standards (IFRS).

Preventing Fraud, Waste, and Abuse: It's Not Just for Accountants Anymore

Internal controls are defined as the policies and procedures set in place to protect the assets and operations of an organization. Internal controls help mitigate the risk of erroneous or unethical transactions from going undetected and ultimately becoming part of the financial statements.

The following questions in Table 10.1 were disseminated to employees of two publicly traded companies to assess the employees' perceptions about their role in upholding the internal controls established by management.

When employees do not feel compelled to uphold either internal controls or a culture characterized by open communication, there is a higher probability that fraud, waste, and abuse can occur.

It is paramount that the HR department continually encourage employees and management of all levels to discuss any concerns they may have about possible fraud, waste, and abuse. Ultimately, even seemingly small infractions of waste of assets in the aggregate can add up to avoidable expenses.

Table 10.1

---

1. All fraudulent activities need to be reported.

☐	☐	☐	☐	☐
STRONGLY AGREE	MILDLY AGREE	UNDECIDED OR UNSURE	MILDLY DISAGREE	STRONGLY DISAGREE

---

2. How familiar are you with the level of materiality or dollar threshold of a transaction that, if erroneous or unethical, must be reported to management?

☐	☐	☐	☐
TO A GREAT EXTENT	TO SOME EXTENT	TO LITTLE EXTENT	NOT AT ALL

---

3. As long as questionable transactions are below materiality (significance) levels, they do not need to be reported to management.

☐	☐	☐	☐	☐
STRONGLY AGREE	MILDLY AGREE	UNDECIDED OR UNSURE	MILDLY DISAGREE	STRONGLY DISAGREE

---

4. It is very important to report any unethical transaction to management.

☐	☐	☐	☐	☐
STRONGLY AGREE	MILDLY AGREE	UNDECIDED OR UNSURE	MILDLY DISAGREE	STRONGLY DISAGREE

---

5. When management promotes an open door, open communication policy, it is more probable that unethical transactions will be reported by employees to management.

☐	☐	☐	☐	☐
STRONGLY AGREE	MILDLY AGREE	UNDECIDED OR UNSURE	MILDLY DISAGREE	STRONGLY DISAGREE

---

6. A corporate culture in which management values its employees' feelings and thoughts helps create a more ethical climate.

☐	☐	☐	☐	☐
STRONGLY AGREE	MILDLY AGREE	UNDECIDED OR UNSURE	MILDLY DISAGREE	STRONGLY DISAGREE

---

7. There will always be questionable transactions that occur which are undetected by management or the auditors of the organization.

☐	☐	☐	☐	☐
STRONGLY AGREE	MILDLY AGREE	UNDECIDED OR UNSURE	MILDLY DISAGREE	STRONGLY DISAGREE

Internal Controls

The following discussions are some of the many types of internal controls. When internal controls are circumvented, the existence of a whistle-blower hotline increases in importance. For example, when any employee witnesses or suspects fraud, he or she should act by anonymously reporting these transactions via the whistle-blower hotline. If and when fraud occurs, human resources would play a critical role in reporting this fraud to the relevant legal authorities for investigation and possible prosecution.

Annual reviews typically are conducted by outside, independent auditors. Auditors cannot be employees of the company, and they must be independent in both fact and appearance. Auditors often examine an organization's internal controls. If internal controls are weak or nonexistent, the auditor is often forced to analyze the source documents and resulting financial statements more closely. This can result in higher audit fees to the organization, but it helps ensure that the audit report/opinion is a true reflection of the financial aspects of the organization.

Human resources must be acutely aware of segregation of duties since without segregation of duties there are more opportunities for unethical behavior, especially with the financial aspect of the business. For example, when one individual opens the mail, records the checks received, makes the bank deposits, and does the bank reconciliation, there is room for manipulation of the funds (i.e., theft or embezzlement). In an era of hiring freezes and expanded duties, segregation of duties is not always possible, but in high risk areas such as cash handling, human resources should establish policies and procedures that seek to segregate the cash handling steps as much as practicable and feasible.

Example: Lack of Rotation of Duties

In this hypothetical example, Sally Harris was the bookkeeper of ABC Company for thirty years. She would bake cookies for the other employees and entertain everyone at work with stories of her grandchildren. Sally was, by all accounts, loyal to the owner of the company. She had thirty years of top-notch annual employee reviews, and she was a productive employee.

Sally's boss, Katyln Booth, was a high-level executive who was often tasked with more responsibilities than normal and who often traveled on company business. Most of Katyln's trips were set up by Sally, and Sally handled the financial end of her boss' travel by submitting the travel vouchers for reimbursement.

Nearly every Friday Sally would ask that the accounting department cut a check for her boss from a previous business trip. This pattern went on for years despite the fact that the company was audited annually.

It was not until Sally had a medical issue and had to take time off for the first time in years that this fraudulent scheme was uncovered. The accounting staff contacted Katyln and asked if she needed her weekly travel reimbursement check. Katyln was astonished and confused by the question since she had not traveled on business for weeks. Sally had stolen this money from her company for years; since she never took time off, no one was aware of the pattern of continuous theft.

The moral of the story: institute policies of segregation of duties and rotation of employees. Human resources can also ensure that all employees take their vacation time and that another employee does the employee's job during the vacation week(s). Human resources can follow up with the employee who has temporarily done the job to see if there are any questionable activities or transactions. Note that it is typically the line manager's responsibility to ensure that the job functions are continued during vacations.

Internal Controls and HR

As mentioned above, part of the function of internal controls is to protect the assets and operations of an organization via adherence to policies and procedures established by management.

Since human resources is management, it is critical that human resources enhances their understanding of internal controls. In many ways, human resources is the voice of senior management.

Communicating and ensuring high levels of compliance with the organization's policies and procedures is a critical aspect of HR's role.

Parallels to Cultural and Change Steward Competency

As mentioned in chapter 2, a critical HR competency has always been to be a steward or protector of an ethical corporate culture. Human resources has always been known for this. HR professionals are the individuals who champion ethical behavior and train all employees in important areas such as the mission of the organization and the code of ethical conduct.

Waste can be defined as using excessive levels or amounts of resources unnecessarily. These resources are typically financial in nature, such as cash or supplies. Waste might include a number of categories, but in essence the focus is on resource misallocation. If employees let the water run in the company kitchen without any thoughts of conservation, this is waste. If employees use excessive amounts of supplies, this is waste. Waste equals higher expenses than necessary. Higher expenses equate to lower net income for the company and its shareholders. Waste hurts everyone in the organization, especially when the company is experiencing a drop in sales or there is an economic recession. When employees do not recognize that they are negatively affecting the long-term financial strength of an organization by fraudulently reporting their business expenses, taking company-owned supplies home with them, or not minimizing other expenses, they are blatantly disregarding their responsibility to help secure the future of their organization. How does this relate to ethical conduct??

Especially in the wake of recent numerous accounting scandals, *it is paramount that human resources take a more active role in upholding an ethical corporate culture.* One suggestion to promote an ethical culture might be to meet with employees on a regular basis to let them know the specifics about the company's code of ethics and the existence of the whistle-blower hotline, as discussed later in this chapter. Human resources can also create hypothetical scenarios in which employees have to assess the most ethical approach to complex business situations. This way, human resources can understand the thought processes of their employees and focus their training on employees' weak areas.

The first line of defense is knowledge of the numerous internal controls that are in place. Depending solely on the accounting staff and upper management is no longer sufficient. Since organizations are increasingly becoming more complex due to mergers and acquisitions, human resources often takes an extremely active role in these organization-wide changes. Human resources needs to be vigilant in upholding the organization's policies, procedures, and ethical culture as the organization evolves.

Circumventing Internal Controls

The business world routinely rediscovers the depth and breadth that management may be willing to go to perpetrate business fraud. So many case studies and books have been written on the ways numerous managers and employees have stolen from their companies that many colleges and universities now have accounting courses about this topic and what the accountant should know.[1]

Sarbanes-Oxley Act Compliance

A code of ethics cannot address all possible situations or dilemmas that can befall dynamic, complex organizations; the code can easily fall short in its intent to convince some employees of what is right or wrong. It is simply a launching point for directing management and employees to do the right thing. Given the interpretative nature of ethics, how can accountants and auditors correctly address the myriad of reporting and auditing situations that occur on a regular basis?[2]

For the provisions of the Sarbanes-Oxley Act (SOX) to be fully executed, no information relating to questionable financial reporting can or should be withheld from management. Compliance with SOX and a strong ethical climate in an organization can create more transparency with the organization's operations and financial reporting.[3]

Rules are simply rules, and they can be circumvented if provisions are not explicitly made to allow for the free flow of information from employees to management. Implicit in this scenario is the existence and promotion of an ethical climate in which there is zero tolerance for unethical or illegal transactions and reporting.[4]

The purpose of SOX is to ensure proper financial reporting through sufficient and reliable internal controls and procedures. The law requires companies to:

- establish good internal controls and procedures;
- certify their completeness and quality;
- file an internal controls report; and
- have an external auditor attest to the sufficiency of the internal controls system

The three objectives of internal controls in a general sense include effectiveness and efficiency of operations, reliability of financial reporting, and compliance with applicable laws and regulations.[5] Human resources is responsible for complying with federal, state, and local laws and regulations related to fraud. We recommend seeking the advice of an attorney who specializes in this area of the law.

In an ideal business environment, there would be no need to mandate compliance with ethical standards that result in the accounting profession maintaining its credible reputation. Instead, accountants would assume the role of protector of the public's interest in ascertaining what is occurring within organizations and ensuring that the financial statements properly reflect an entity's financial operations. Complacency is a real threat to the necessary vigilance of upholding high ethical standards and procedures.[6] Another threat is not really having high ethical standards and procedures.

HR's Role in Upholding Internal Controls and an Ethical Culture

Human resources should be highly visible to their organization's employees and management on a daily basis. Human resources should be available. Human resources should strive to have an open-door policy and regularly remind employees to drop by to talk about any work-related issues or concerns. Being proactive rather than reactive with any organizational issues or challenges will make resolution of those issues that much easier.

Training seminars, webinars, newsletters, emails, and blogs are some of the many ways that employees can hear from human resources about compliance with internal controls and the critical nature of upholding an ethical corporate culture.

HR as a Partner in the First Line of Defense

Many business experts contend that human resources is the first defense against financial fraud within their organizations. Knowing the warning signs can make all the difference. Knowing who to report concerns to regarding potential fraud is also key. Many organizations have an audit committee, and human resources can report any suspicious behavior to this group. In lieu of an audit committee, the board members should be told of questionable activities.

In the article, "HR and Accounting: What the HR Professional Needs to Know," the authors challenge old stereotypes that accounting and finance department employees are numbers people and HR employees are soft skills people.[7]

Some of the areas in which both employee groups can and should work together include:

- Budgeting and forecasting (see chapter 8);
- Analysis of employee productivity;
- Implementing and monitoring internal controls (discussed in chapter 10);
- Indentifying and preventing fraud; and

• Establishing employee benefit programs.

Given the very existence of criminal behavior, others assert that legislation rarely prevents unethical acts or immoral behavior.[8] Instead, legislation only allows for mechanisms for dealing with such behavior while corporate culture is the "muscle" behind how an organization trains its employees. This unique organizational perspective and approach can affect how ethical dilemmas and issues are resolved within the organization.

Legislation is comparable to workplace policies and procedures—these too cannot by virtue of their existence stop negative employee behavior.

Fraud: The Highest Level of Deception

Some types of unethical behavior may be explained away by some employees, although not for the HR professional, since ethics can be interpretative. The discussion of ethics in great detail is beyond the scope of this book, but suffice it to say that ethics and the discussion thereof is a huge part of accounting.

Erroneous reporting of transactions is often a result of poor internal controls. This unintentional misrepresentation of accounting and business information is quite common. Auditors find some but not all erroneous transaction reporting, so it is up to human resources, along with employees and other managers, to promote and secure an ethical corporate culture.

Under common law, three elements are required to prove fraud:

1. a material false statement
2. made with an intent to deceive (scienter)
3. victim's reliance on the statement and damages.

Certainly there have always been opportunities for fraud in business. What differs today from a century ago is that increasingly complex business structures allow for higher levels of potential concealment of unethical decisions. As an examination of accounting history will reveal, the interests of managers often do not coincide with those of the corporation owners or shareholders.[9]

Today, complex, multifaceted organizations that are growing at an unprecedented rate via mergers, acquisitions, and joint ventures can easily obscure unethical behaviors similar to Enron if both internal and external controls are weak or nonexistent. There is also not a clear distinction between what is legal and what is ethical.[10]

Two Types of Financial Fraud

The two primary categories of financial fraud are *misappropriation of assets* (i.e., employee fraud) and *fraudulent financial reporting* (i.e., management fraud). Collusion at the top is the most challenging type of fraud to detect because it means that two or more members of management are working together to defraud the organization. Even for highly trained financial auditors, it is very difficult to detect collusion at the top. When there are several managers working together to hide fraudulent activities, auditors are unlikely to be able to easily detect these illegal activities. Many of the recent high-profile fraud cases have been management fraud cases.[11]

Management is responsible for designing, implementing, maintaining, and enforcing a system of controls to prevent misappropriation of assets.

Anti-Fraud Programs Triangle

Human resources must be aware of the interaction of the three aspects of preventing fraud since it should be a driving force behind promoting an ethical culture. It may have to discipline or fire employees who act inappropriately. The Anti-Fraud Programs triangle has three components that overlap. They are:

• Prevention, which means stopping something from occurring in the first place

- Detection, which can be described as discovering the existence of something
- Deterrence, which can be defined as discouraging or restraining from acting or continuing

The Fraud Triangle

As illustrated in Figure 10.1, this often-cited fraud triangle includes three aspects or characteristics that drive the individual to perform illegal acts.

Figure 10.1 The Fraud Triangle

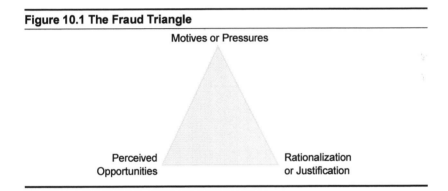

The anti-fraud triangle depicts ways to prevent fraud within an organization and the fraud triangle focuses on what drives individuals to act fraudulently. Human resources can play a critical role in indentifying individuals who are exhibiting some of these characteristics. There is a substantial difference between pressure to commit fraud and normal workplace pressure. For example, lower-paid employees experiencing a life change such as marriage or parenthood might be looking for ways to increase their access to cash. Fraud can happen at all employee levels.

Human resources can also help prevent some types of fraud by ensuring the rotation of auditors and through oversight of interactions between auditors and management. Auditors must be independent and must not become too friendly or interactive with management. If and when fraud is detected, human resources can also communicate concerns with the audit committee (if one exists) or the board of directors.

Human resources needs to be aware of some warning signs that fraudulent behavior may be taking place. For example, if management's bonuses are solely tied to quarterly earnings and the company has been performing poorly in sales recently, management members who are underpaid (and thereby feel entitled to padding their pockets) or who have excessive power and access to the financial information may have more opportunities than usual in "cooking the books." Also, if earnings per share have been at a certain level for many years and there is a sudden increase, human resources may join forces with the audit committee or auditors to investigate why earnings exceeded expectations during a downturn in the economy.

When there are relaxed internal controls or lack of formal training of employees regarding those internal controls (i.e., policies and procedures), there may be more opportunity to manipulate the financial results of an organization. This can be especially difficult to detect if some of these individuals are members of management.

Open-Door Policy

Policies and procedures, including internal controls, cannot overcome a corporate culture that does not value open communication and self-correction. (Self-correction means that financial transactions that are recorded erroneously must be corrected by employees rather than auditors.) What often happens within organizations that do not promote open lines of communication is that individuals who are courageous enough to come forward to report questionable practices are not only rebuked, but management can thwart their efforts. Changing this key aspect within an organization can mean a monumental difference between self-correction of unethical practices and the possibility that whistleblowing will ultimately become necessary.

Whistle-blower Hotlines

Whistle-blower hotlines are required to be set up by publicly traded companies as a way for employees, or anyone associated with the company, to anonymously report fraudulent activity to the company. No repercussions can occur that are detrimental to the individual reporting the fraud, per the whistle-blower provision of SOX. Many other non-publicly traded companies have chosen to implement an anonymous hotline even though they are not required to do so per the Act.

It has been reported that the level of usage of an anonymous hotline is more dependent on the user's perceptions of anonymity than claims of the communication channel actually being anonymous.[13]

Unfortunately, one of Congress' oversights in the whistle-blowing component of SOX is that despite the requirement that companies must establish a hotline for receiving anonymous reports of possible questionable accounting or auditing practices, there is no requirement to communicate its existence to employees or provide training on how to use such a system.

Companies differ in how aggressively they combat possible fraud.[14] Those that have been "at the forefront of fraud prevention will, among other things, restrict employment of ineligible persons; hire a compliance officer and/or appoint a compliance committee; publish a set of values that reflect the expectation of ethical work practices; train employees in how to implement the company's ethics code; and provide ongoing training in fraud detection and prevention."[15]

International Financial Reporting Standards

Over the past few years a set of global accounting standards (International Financial Reporting Standards, or IFRS) has been developed, and more than 100 countries currently use these rules. The European Union (EU) adopted IFRS in 2005. There is increasing pressure on the United States (which currently uses "Generally Accepted Accounting Principles," or GAAP) to adopt IFRS, and this change would have far-reaching effects on all publicly traded companies.

Multi-national companies are governed by an extensive set of accounting guidelines and rules. Development of these rules has been an arduous, painstaking effort on the part of accounting standards boards around the world. U.S. companies that own foreign subsidiaries in countries that have already adopted IFRS, such as countries in the EU, have to produce financial statements using both GAAP and IFRS.

The HR professional needs to be aware that there could be substantial strategic planning needs and opportunities for organizations that will have to adopt this sweeping accounting change. First and foremost, human resources needs to realize that this transition to IFRS from GAAP is most likely inevitable for publicly traded companies.

The adoption of IFRS will directly affect human resources. For example, management of all levels will have to be trained on IFRS once the decision is made by the Securities and Exchange Commission, among others, to adopt IFRS.

Consider the following quote, which addresses the general concept of the massive undertaking of training employees on the concept of IFRS. In effect, what is being stated is that accountants have not shared their knowledge with their colleagues when it came to accounting standards and rules. This *must* change if and when IFRS is adopted since the entire organization will be affected. The areas affected will include information systems, internal controls, tax, and the necessity of educating investors on what the changes mean to them.

It has been suggested that companies

"Create a steering committee and core project team. The steering committee should be comprised of senior management from accounting, tax, communications, human resources, investor relations, legal, information systems, manufacturing and sales. The dedicated core team will identify technical accounting differences, draft the corporate accounting manual, interact with external auditors, work with information systems to design the system reporting requirements and conduct global training programs."[16]

Human resources will also have to hire accountants who are trained on IFRS. Beginning in January 2011, the CPA exam content and skill specifications will require an advanced understanding of differences between GAAP and IFRS. Human resources should not make the assumption that if an accountant passes the CPA exam after 2011 and can answer a small number of questions related to IFRS that this accountant is highly knowledgeable about IFRS. So if human resources interviews and/or hires CPAs who have passed the exam in 2011, then they may partially meet the "prepared" expectation.

Human resources may want to collaborate with colleagues whose companies have already adopted IFRS to see how those companies went through this lengthy transition.

Proactive Approaches from the HR Perspective

One goal that you may want to consider is to become an informed individual about the timeframes in which IFRS will apply to your organization and to start having conversations about this now with top management. Read everything you can about this worldwide accounting change. You do not have to read about the details, but be aware of major changes or legislation that relates to the accounting and finance aspects of your organization.

Option two is to wait until your organization makes this transition to IFRS and send your accounting and management staff for training. CPA firms and organizations like the American Management Association are actively involved in creating and promoting many training opportunities for publicly traded companies that anticipate having to comply with IFRS.

Legislative Acts and Strategy Architect Parallels

It is not just wise but also imperative that human resources take an active role in assisting management in preparing for this monumental change from GAAP to IFRS. Approach the situation as an opportunity to illustrate your business acumen.

Specifically, as a Strategy Architect the HR professional should consider the following actions in order to make this overwhelming transition a little less stressful for all involved:

- Investigate the various options available for training current accounting staff and management
- Request budgeting information for these training sessions if done by outside vendors
- Before hiring new accountants, research which universities have courses on IFRS (currently there are few, but that could easily change in the next couple of years)
- Create an inter-departmental task force that would research and discuss financial ramifications of IFRS implementation
- Enhance and encourage open dialogue between the HR department and management

What You Should Know

- Human resources plays an important role in preventing fraud, waste, and abuse.
- Internal controls are policies and procedures established to protect a company's assets and operations. There are numerous types of internal controls.
- Internal controls can be circumvented by management.
- For publicly traded companies, IFRS is coming. Sending your accounting and management staff to training is critical.
- During the transition period to using IFRS, two sets of financial statements will have to be created: one using U.S. GAAP and one using IFRS.
- Not all companies will have to transition to IFRS. Currently only publicly traded companies will have to deal with this compliance issue.
- For hiring purposes, the number of accountants with IFRS knowledge will initially most likely be small.

Conclusion

Throughout this book you read about many business terms and examples as they relate to you in the HR profession. Keep this book on your desk and use it as both a reference book with terms you need to review and a daily guide to help you, the HR professional, develop and maintain your enhanced role as a strategic partner.

Fundamental Concepts to Know Well

It is suggested that you be very well-informed and familiar with at least these topics listed below. If you can explain to another individual both the overall and details on these topics, your time invested in learning them is immeasurable. Some aspects of these topics will be more important to you than others, depending on your background and your career choice within your organization.

- Interpretation and understanding of the financial statements
- Understanding of financial ratios
- Knowledge of internal controls as they relate to human resources
- HR competencies (per Dave Ulrich) as they relate to business literacy

Concepts and Terms to Refer to as Necessary

- Differences between cash and accrual accounting
- Capital structure
- Budgeting

- Legislative acts such as the Sarbanes-Oxley Act and International Financial Reporting Standards
- Cash flow statement specifics

Return on Investment

In the preface, we discussed return on investment (ROI) for the HR professional. What could you expect to learn, and how would this knowledge help you now and in the future? The following list is not exhaustive, but it serves as a starting place to summarize some of the important features of this book. Circling back to the many facets of ROI listed in the preface is appropriate at this time.

Consider the concepts discussed in this book, highlighting the following:

- Understanding financial stability of your organization: stocks, bonds, other debt, earnings per share, and trend analysis
- Analyzing the potential growth of your organization via cash management, the cash flow statement, financial ratios, net income, the balance sheet, and discussion of mergers and acquisitions
- Taking on an enhanced and more active role in minimizing fraud, waste, and abuse by understanding major financial risks such as earnings management
- Internalizing the ways HR competencies are related to business literacy using examples described throughout the book
- Understanding internal controls as they relate to HR's role in upholding an ethical corporate culture
- Becoming familiar with management's fiduciary role as the agent of shareholders and management's responsibility to increase shareholders' investments by growing the company
- Understanding accruals and estimates and use of judgment in accounting
- Utilizing strengths, weaknesses, opportunities, and threats (SWOT) analysis as a management tool

- Understanding how an organization's goals and objectives drive the strategic plan
- Appreciating auditors' roles within and outside the organization and the risks they evaluate

Business Literacy Survey

The following charts and graphs came from my research in 2009 with one mid-Atlantic SHRM group that graciously complied with my request to complete an online business literacy survey. The results are remarkable. It is possible that some HR professionals surprised themselves in either a good way or a bad way about their level of expertise in financial matters.

The most telling aspect of the short survey is that 105 individuals started the survey but for some questions, a much smaller number of survey participants answered some particular questions. The non-completion of the entire survey could be due to frustration vs. lack of time or the length of the survey.

Some of the results of the survey follow.

Business Literacy Basics 2009		
Please describe your level of expertise in business literacy.		
Answer Options	**Response Percent**	**Response Count**
Expert in financial aspects	1.9%	2
Very familiar with some financial aspects	23.8%	25
Somewhat familiar with some financial aspects	58.1%	61
Not that familiar with financial aspects	16.2%	17
	answered question	105
	skipped question	0

Please describe your level of expertise in business literacy.

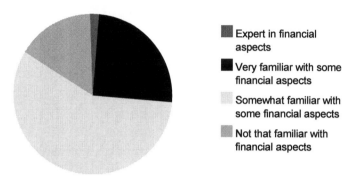

- Expert in financial aspects
- Very familiar with some financial aspects
- Somewhat familiar with some financial aspects
- Not that familiar with financial aspects

Which Financial Statement(s) do you have a working knowledge or understanding of:

Answer Options	Response Percent	Response Count
Income Statement	69.7%	62
Statement of Owners' Equity or RE	21.3%	19
Balance Sheet	70.8%	63
Statement of Cash Flows	36.0%	32
None of the above	20.2%	18
answered question		89
skipped question		16

Business Literacy Basics 2009

The components of the Balance Sheet are:

Answer Options	Response Percent	Response Count
revenue and expenses	21.3%	19
assets, liabilities and revenue	29.2%	26
assets, liabilities and owners' equity	49.4%	44
cash from operating and financing activities	0.0%	0
answered question		89
skipped question		16

This is interesting because almost 71 percent of the respondents for the previous question said they were familiar with the balance sheet, but only 49 percent got the question correct about the components of the balance sheet.

The components of the Balance Sheet are:

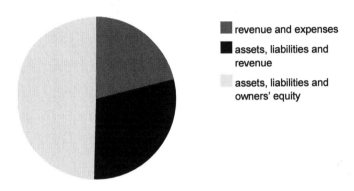

- revenue and expenses
- assets, liabilities and revenue
- assets, liabilities and owners' equity

The correct answer for the components of the Balance Sheet is: assets, liabilities, and owners' equity.

Financial Ratios express the relationship between two numbers and if you are able to calculate and interpret some ratios from each of the four classifications of ratios, the job of analyzing the financial statements can be accomplished more thoroughly. Please note which ratios you are familiar with:

Answer Options	Response Percent	Response Count
Liquidity ratios including the current ratio, quick ratio	23.1%	12
Profitability ratios including operating margin and return on total assets	26.9%	14
Asset Management ratios including total asset turnover and age of facility ratio	21.2%	11
Debt management ratios including LT debt to net assets and times interest earned ratio	19.2%	10
None of the above	59.6%	31
	answered question	52
	skipped question	53

How familiar are you with the following types of budgets:

Answer Options	Very familiar	Familiar	Somewhat familiar	Not familiar	Response Count
Operating budget	14	16	19	8	57
Cash budget	6	12	20	17	55
Capital budget	6	13	17	20	56
	26	41	56	45	
				answered question	57
				skipped question	48

Business Literary Glossary

Accelerated Depreciation Method: A greater percentage of depreciation expense is taken in the early years of the life of an asset than in the later years.

Accounting: The systematic process of identifying, recording, measuring, and reporting financial transactions of a business.

Accounts Payable Turnover Ratio: The rate at which suppliers are paid (Cost of Goods Sold + Average Accounts Payable).

Accounts Payable: When the business owes other vendors or businesses for services or products purchased.

Accounts Receivable Turnover Ratio: Indicates how quickly or efficiently customers are being billed and their payments collected (Revenue + Average Accounts Receivable).

Accounts Receivable: When customers purchase "on account" and are billed and pay the business later or over time.

Accrual Basis/Method Accounting: Transactions are recorded regardless of when cash will be received or paid. This applies to revenue earned and expenses incurred.

Accruals: Used to match revenue and expenses in the same period.

Accumulated Depreciation: The total amount of depreciation for both the current and prior years. It cannot exceed the cost of the asset. It belongs on the balance sheet.

Activity Based Costing: The identification of key activities that cause costs to be incurred. These activities are called cost drivers.

Allocation of Overhead Expenses: Companies allocate some overhead expenses such as the CEO's salary and building costs to internal departments based on certain criteria. The criteria that can be used to allocate these overhead, fixed costs to departments can be labor hours per department or a percentage of the building used per department.

Assets: Things that are owned (e.g., cash, accounts receivable, supplies, equipment, land, and buildings).

Audit: A systematic examination and verification of an organization's transaction records, financial statements, and other relevant documents to render an opinion as to whether the statements are fairly represented.

Average Accounts Payable: The entire amount of accounts payable for the year, divided by 360 days.

Average Accounts Receivable: The entire amount of the accounts receivable for the year, divided by 360 days.

Average Costs: Costs are lumped together and then divided by some measure such as quantity of output.

Average Inventory: The entire amount of inventory for the year, divided by 360 days.

Avoidable Costs: Variable costs that may be avoided if a particular course of action is not taken. Fixed costs are usually unavoidable in the short run.

Bad Debt Expenses: An estimate (a) of the percentage of net sales that won't be collectible from customers or (b) the percentage of accounts receivable that won't be collectible.

Balance Sheet: The amount of assets, liabilities, and capital at any moment in time (Assets = Total liabilities + Capital).

Bankruptcy, Chapter 11: The type of bankruptcy in which the organization continues to exist after completing the procedure.

Bankruptcy, Chapter 7: The type of bankruptcy in which the organization ceases to exist once all claims have been paid.

Bondholders: An individual or organization that owns a bond.

Bondholders Interest: This type of interest income is distributed to bondholders (owners) as a way to compensate them for purchasing the bond.

Bonds: A certificate that represents an organization's promise to pay a certain amount of money and interest in the future. Bonds are a form of debt to the organization selling the bond.

Bottom Line: This is an informal description of net income or net loss, the difference between revenue and expenses on the income statement.

Break-even Point: The point (in units sold or in revenue) when there is neither a profit nor a loss.

Budgets: A budget is a financial document used to project future income and expenses. The budgeting process helps an organization estimate if it can continue to operate with its projected income and expenses. There are numerous types of budgets.

Burn Rate: The timeframe in which a company uses cash-on-hand.

Capital: The amount invested into the business by the shareholders or owner(s) of a business. Ownership interest in a corporation in the form of common stock or preferred stock (same as equity).

Capital Budget: An estimate of company needs in regard to fixed assets.

Capital Expenditures: Long-term investments for assets such as buildings or equipment.

Capital Leases: Leases that transfer ownership of an asset eventually to the renter. The asset that is being leased is listed on the balance sheet.

Capital Loans: Often called working capital loans, are funds borrowed by a business that needs cash to keep growing or to cover some operating expenses. Without a working capital loan some businesses are unable to generate enough revenue to stay afloat.

Capitalize: To write it off (depreciate it) an asset over a number of years.

Cash: Cash, coins, customer checks, petty cash and money orders held by an organization.

Cash Basis Financial Reporting: A system of accounting in which revenues are recognized only when cash is received and expenses are recognized only when cash is paid.

Cash Dividends: The distribution of company profits paid in cash to shareholders (stockholders).

Cash Flow Budget: An estimate of future cash receipts and expenditures for a particular time period. It helps the business determine when income will be sufficient to cover expenses and when the company will need to seek outside financing.

Cash Management: The timing of inflows and outflows of cash within an organization.

Collection Period Ratio: Determines the average number of days in which customers pay the business of services rendered ((Average Accounts Receivable x 360) + Sales).

Collusion at the Top: When two or more top managers commit fraud together.

Common Stock: The most common type of stock. Common stockholders are permitted to vote at annual shareholder meetings.

Contributed Capital: This would include money generated from the sale of stock such as common and possibly preferred stock.

Convertibles: Investments that can be changed into shares of stock.

Corporation: Companies that meets certain legal requirements. Corporations are separate and distinct from their owners. Corporations are owned by their shareholders (stockholders) who share in profits and losses generated through the company's operations. Corporations have limited liability to creditors.

Cost Drivers: Essential business activities that incur a cost.

Cost of Goods Sold (COGS): The cost of a product to the organization, which may be sold later for a profit. It is shown on the income statement as a deduction.

Cost-Benefit Analysis: Helps in analyzing whether an investment is worthwhile; i.e., whether the benefits derived from the investment will outweigh the costs of engaging in the investment.

Credit(s): The right side of a T-Account. Certain accounts increase with a credit: liabilities, revenue, and capital.

Creditors: Either an individual or organization to which the company owes a debt.

Current Asset: An asset that is expected to be realized in cash or sold or consumed during the operating cycle of the organization or within one year, whichever is shorter.

Current Liability: A financial obligation that will be satisfied within the next operating cycle or within one year if the cycle is shorter than one year.

Current Ratio: A simple liquidity ratio (Current Assets ÷ Current Liabilities).

Debit(s): The left side of a T-Account. Certain accounts increase with debits: assets, withdraws/dividends, and expenses.

Debt: A financial obligation that must be repaid.

Debt/Equity Ratio: A leverage ratio that indicates how much of a company is financed by debt rather than by its owners/shareholders ((Short-term Debt + Long-term debt) ÷ Total Equity).

Depreciation: Writing off the cost of an asset gradually, over its estimated useful life. It is an expense on the income statement. As depreciation expenses "accumulate" they are also shown on the balance sheet as accumulated depreciation.

Depreciation Expense: This is the portion of the depreciation deducted for the current year. Depreciation expense is shown on the income statement. See *Depreciation*.

Dividends: Monies that are distributed to shareholders of a corporation. Dividends are distributions to shareholders who often purchase stock for their cash generating potential. Shareholders often purchase stock specifically with the expectation of receiving dividends as income. Some shareholders reinvest their dividends in order to purchase more shares of stock in the company. In theory, a company should distribute some of the company's earnings in the form of dividends unless there are business reasons such as future expansion or asset replacement that require them not to pay a dividend.

Dividends in Arrears: Preferred shareholders who own cumulative preferred stock are entitled to receive dividends in future years if the company cannot pay them their dividend in the current year.

Double Declining Balance (DDB) Method: This depreciation method, also known as the 200 percent declining balance method of depreciation, is a common form of *accelerated* depreciation. See *Accelerated Depreciation Method*. Although the depreciation will be faster, the *total* depreciation over the life of the asset will not be greater than the *total* depreciation using the straight line method.

Double-entry Accounting: When, during the typical financial transaction, at least two account categories are impacted.

Earnings: This is often another way of describing net income (revenue less expenses).

Earnings Management: The manipulation of income into the timeframe which is most beneficial to management.

Earnings per Share Ratio (EPS): Indicates the shareholders' part of the earnings after taxes ((Earnings after taxes - Preferred dividends) ÷ Weighted Average of Shares Outstanding).

Economic Order Quantity (EOQ): A formula used to calculate the optimal level of inventory.

Equity: See *Capital*.

Expenses: The costs of doing business (e.g., rent, commissions, and salaries).

Fiduciary: An individual in whom another has placed the utmost trust and confidence or a person who holds assets in trust for a beneficiary.

Financial Instrument: An instrument having monetary value or recording a monetary transaction. Examples could include cash and cash equivalents, but also securities such as bonds and stocks that have value.

Financial Statements: A written report that quantitatively describes the financial health of a company. Examples include the income statement, statement of retained earnings or owners' equity, the balance sheet, and the statement of cash flows.

Financial Transactions: Accounting or financial transactions are the components of an accounting system that keeps track of changes in accounts that affect an organization. For every transaction that gets recorded, one or more debits and one or more credits are used.

Fixed Assets: A long-term, tangible asset held for business use and not expected to be converted to cash in the current or upcoming year. Examples include manufacturing equipment, buildings and furniture.

Fixed Costs: Expenses that occur and have to be paid regardless of the level of output.

Fixed Overhead Costs: According to cost accounting theory, this involves costs such as rent, insurance, and the CEO's salary that do not change as sales volume or production volumes change.

Flexible Budget: Compares actual results with budgeted numbers and is based on more than one activity.

Fraud: An intentional, illegal act. Revenue recognition fraud is the most prevalent type of financial statement fraud committed. This type of fraud can involve the recording of fictitious revenue, or recording revenue not yet earned or received.

Free Cash Flow: The cash left over after the organization has paid all of its expenses, including investments.

Future Value (FV): Future value measures the future sum of money that a given amount of money is "worth" at a specified time in the future assuming a certain interest rate. Inflation is ignored for FV calculations.

General and Administrative Expenses: Normal operating expenses of an organization.

Generally Accepted Accounting Principles (GAAP): The GAAP hierarchy consists of the sources of accounting principles used in the preparation of financial statements of federal reporting entities that are presented in conformity with GAAP and the framework for selecting those principles (www.aicpa.org). These accounting rules are used in the United States.

Gross Margin: The difference between sales revenue and cost of goods sold (COGS).

Gross Profit Margin: The percentage of sales that is left over after deducting cost of goods sold ((Sales - Cost of Goods Sold) ÷ Sales).

Gross Profit Ratio: See *Gross Profit Margin*.

Income Statement: The operating activities of a company. Contains revenue and expenses.

Incremental Analysis: Evaluating financial data that changes under different courses of action.

Institutional Investors: They are organizations that pool large sums of money and invest those sums in securities, real property and other investment assets.

Interest Expenses: The cost of borrowing money. It is affected by the interest rate and length of the loan or other form of debt.

Internal Controls: The processes and procedures used to help lessen the chances and magnitude of fraud, waste, and abuse.

Internal Rate of Return (IRR) Method: Is a tool to measure and compare the profitability of investments.

International Financial Reporting Standards (IFRS): A global set of accounting standards not yet adopted in the United States but, as of the printing of this book, already adopted in over 100 countries worldwide.

Inventory: These are goods and materials (parts of the goods). They are often those items held available in stock by a business.

Inventory Equation: Explains inventory flows (Beginning Inventory + Net Purchases - Cost of Goods Sold = Ending Inventory).

Inventory Purchases Budget: An estimate for the purchasing inventory for resale.

Inventory Turnover Ratio: Indicates how well an organization manages its inventory levels (Cost of Goods Sold ÷ Average Inventory).

Investors: A party or individual that makes investment into certain assets, i.e., part of a company, real estate, etc.

IRS Form 1099: Tax form used for independent contractors or consultants to report revenue earned by individuals who are not W-2 employees.

Leverage Ratios: Measures the amount of debt that exists on the balance sheet.

Liabilities: What is owed by the business and to be paid to others such as other companies or the bank (e.g., accounts payable and notes payable).

Limited Liability: This is a major advantage that certain types of companies have in which there is a legal separation between shareholders and the company. This ensures that if the company were to be sued, the most money the shareholders can lose is up to their dollar investment.

Limited Liability Company (LLC): A type of company, authorized only in certain states, in which owners and managers receive the limited liability and (usually) tax benefits of an S Corporation without having to conform to the S corporation restrictions.

Liquidity: The ease in which assets can be turned into cash. Liquid assets include cash, accounts receivable, and inventory.

Liquidity Ratios: Addresses the ability of the organization to pay its short-term financial obligations.

Marginal Costs: The cost from the last unit produced.

Marginal Revenue: Revenue from the last unit sold.

Marketing Budget: An estimate of the funds needed for promotion, advertising, and public relations.

Materials Purchases Budget: This budget is used in companies producing tangible goods. This budget contains materials used and their costs to the company.

Net Income: Revenue less expenses; the "bottom line."

Net Present Value Method: An approach that focuses on the time value of money to analyze the viability of a capital project.

Notes Payable: This written promise to pay a debt is called a "promissory note." They are long-term loans, sometimes known as a loan note or an I.O.U. Most often a promissory note is typically written or prepared by an attorney, bank or lending institution.

Operating Expenses: These expenses are expenses incurred by an organization that relate to daily operations. They include subtotals of selling expenses and general and administrative expenses.

Operating Leases: Through the lease the renter will not eventually own the asset that is being rented.

Operating Margin Ratio: What a company makes in profit after paying variable costs.

Operational/Efficiency Ratios: Efficiency ratios can reflect how well an organization plans and controls financing and use of its assets.

Overhead Expenses: Expenses that exist regardless of how much or little the company earns in terms of sales of either products or services (e.g., utilities and rent).

Owner's Equity Statement: Tracks the amount that the owner(s) have invested into the business.

Par Value: An arbitrary value given to the stock in a company's corporate charter.

Partnership: An unincorporated entity that is owned by two or more partners. Characteristics include unlimited liability and mutual agency, which means that one partner can represent and make decisions for all other partners.

Payback Method: Analyzes how quickly extra money into the organization occurs as a result of the investment, compared to the initial cost of the investment.

Preferred Stock: Stock owned by preferred shareholders. Preferred stock characteristics do not include the right to vote on company issues but does include priority in receiving dividends before common shareholders.

Present Value (PV): The value of money in today's terms and relevant to capital budgeting.

Price-Earnings Ratio (P/E): Measure of the price paid per share relative to the net income or profit earned per share.

Pro Forma: Means "projected."

Production Budget: An estimate of the number of units that must be manufactured and their associated costs in order to meet the sales goals.

Profitability: The ability to earn a profit, i.e., when revenue exceeds expenses.

Project Budget: An estimate of the costs associated with a particular company project.

Purpose of the Statement of Cash Flows: To explain in detail the change in the balance sheet cash balance from last year to this year.

Quick Ratio: An advanced liquidity ratio ((Cash + Accounts Receivable + Short-term Securities) ÷ Current Liabilities).

Relevant Costs: Costs that can change a decision.

Retained Earnings: The current and previous organizational level earnings that are kept in the organization in order for it to grow or expand.

Return on Equity (ROE): A measurement of how a company is using investor money Traditional formula: Net Profit After Taxes ÷ Stockholders' Equity; DuPont Formula: (Net Profit After Taxes ÷ Total Assets) × (Total Assets ÷ Stockholders' Equity).

Return on Investment (ROI): A performance measurement used to evaluate the efficiency of an investment.

Revenue: The sales generated from either a service or sale of a product.

Reverse Stock Splits: When company stock price decreases significantly, a company can institute a reverse stock split so there is a proportionate decrease in the *number* of shares, but not the total *value* of shares of stock held by shareholders. Shareholders maintain the same percentage of equity as before the split. For example, a 1-for-2 split would result in stockholders owning one share for every two shares owned before the split. A firm generally institutes a reverse split to increase its stock's market price.

Risk: The quantifiable possibility of loss or less-than-expected returns. Examples: currency risk, inflation risk, principal risk, country risk, economic risk, mortgage risk, liquidity risk, market risk, etc.

Rolling Budget: Prepared for several future periods and revised several times prior to the budget period.

Sales Budget: An estimate of future sales in units and dollars.

Sarbanes-Oxley Act (SOX): The purpose of the law is to ensure proper financial reporting through sufficient and reliable internal controls and procedures, including a whistle-blower protection.

Securities: Financing or investment instruments (some negotiable, others not) bought and sold in financial markets. Examples may include bonds, notes, options and shares of stocks.

Self-correction: Financial transactions, which are recorded erroneously, must be corrected by employees rather than by auditors.

Shareholders: Stockholders or owners of shares of the company. Shareholders can be either common or preferred shareholders.

Short-term Securities: securities with a maturity of one year or less, such as money market instruments.

Single-period Budget: Prepared only once prior to the budget period.

Sole Proprietorship: A type of entity with one owner that is easy to form and has unlimited liability. See *Unlimited Liability*.

Solvency: The ability of an organization to pay its long-term financial obligations.

Statement of Cash Flow: The financial statement done on the cash vs. accrual basis that is the most complex of the four financial statements. It can be described as "sources and uses of cash," and it reconciles the beginning and ending balances of cash on the balance sheet.

Statement of Retained Earnings: This financial statement is done after the income statement and the statement of retained earnings contains beginning retained earnings plus income (or minus net loss) minus dividends.

Static Budgets: Shows one level of activity and works best when the planned level of activity is the same as the actual level of activity.

Stock Dividends: The distribution of company profits paid in stock distributed to shareholders instead of cash dividends.

Stock Out: When a company is running out of salable inventory.

Stock Splits: When company stock gets too costly for many investors, the company makes the determination to split the stock into more shares. After a split, the number of shares increases and the price of each share decreases. The market capitalization stays the same.

Stocks: Pro rata (proportionate) ownership of a company. Shareholders purchase company stock, thereby becoming the owners of that company.

Straight Line Depreciation: Simplest form of depreciation. After calculating the depreciation expense for the first year, the same amount for the expense is used every year of the asset's estimated useful life.

Time Value of Money: Related to the value of money increasing over time.

Total Debt Ratio: A leverage ratio that indicates the level or percentage of assets that are financed through debt (Total Liabilities ÷ Total Assets).

Trend Analysis: Analyzes particular items (e.g., orders, hiring, cost-increases) over several years to discern patterns that will assist in decision-making.

Unlimited Liability: A characteristic of some forms of partnerships and of sole proprietorships in that if the entity gets sued, the owner(s) can lose not only their investments in the business but all or part of their personal assets.

Vacation Benefits Expenses: A company's expense for its employees' paid vacations. An organization normally accrues for this expense as employees gradually earn this benefit by earning their wages.

Value Stock: Underpriced stock that is assumed to appreciate or increase in value over time.

Variable Costs: Costs that vary up or down depending on production levels. Examples can include labor or materials used directly in production of the product.

Variable Overhead Costs: Manufacturing overhead costs that vary with output.

Variance: The difference between actual costs and expected costs.

Warranty Expenses: Expenses recorded by an organization when the product is sold vs. when the warranty gets used. Warranty expenses are normally a percentage of sales, i.e., 2 percent of sales are recorded as warranty expenses.

Waste: Inefficient use of resources. Waste can equate to higher expenses and should be minimized.

Weighted Average of Shares Outstanding: More weight is given to shares owned for longer periods of time.

Withdrawals: Cash taken out of the business if the business is a sole proprietorship.

Working Capital Ratio: Used to determine the ability to pay short-term liabilities (Current Assets - Current Liabilities).

Write Off: Deducting the cost of an asset gradually or eliminating items such as uncollectible accounts receivable.

Zero-based Budgeting: Prioritizes and justifies departmental activities.

Form 1099-MISC

Attention:

This form is provided for informational purposes only. Copy A appears in red, similar to the official IRS form. Do **not** file copy A downloaded from this website. The official printed version of this IRS form is scannable, but the online version of it, printed from this website, is not. A penalty of $50 per information return may be imposed for filing forms that cannot be scanned.

To order official IRS forms, call 1-800-TAX-FORM (1-800-829-3676) or Order Information Returns and Employer Returns Online, and we'll mail you the scannable forms and other products.

See IRS Publications 1141, 1167, 1179 and other IRS resources for information about printing these tax forms.

9595 ☐ VOID ☐ CORRECTED

PAYER'S name, street address, city, state, ZIP code, and telephone no.		1 Rents	OMB No. 1545-0115	
		$	**2010**	Miscellaneous Income
		2 Royalties		
		$	Form 1099-MISC	
		3 Other income	4 Federal income tax withheld	Copy A
		$	$	For
PAYER'S federal identification number	RECIPIENT'S identification number	5 Fishing boat proceeds	6 Medical and health care payments	Internal Revenue Service Center
		$	$	File with Form 1096.
RECIPIENT'S name		7 Nonemployee compensation	8 Substitute payments in lieu of dividends or interest	For Privacy Act and Paperwork Reduction Act
		$	$	Notice, see the
Street address (including apt. no.)		9 Payer made direct sales of $5,000 or more of consumer products to a buyer (recipient) for resale ▶ ☐	10 Crop insurance proceeds	2010 General Instructions for
			$	Certain
City, state, and ZIP code		11	12	Information
Account number (see instructions)	2nd TIN not.	13 Excess golden parachute payments	14 Gross proceeds paid to an attorney	Returns.
	☐	$	$	
15a Section 409A deferrals	15b Section 409A income	16 State tax withheld	17 State/Payer's state no.	18 State income
$	$	$		$
		$		$

Form **1099-MISC**   Cat. No. 14425J   Department of the Treasury - Internal Revenue Service

Do Not Cut or Separate Forms on This Page — Do Not Cut or Separate Forms on This Page

☐ VOID   ☐ CORRECTED

PAYER'S name, street address, city, state, ZIP code, and telephone no.		1 Rents $	OMB No. 1545-0115	Miscellaneous
		2 Royalties $	2010	Income
		3 Other income $	Form 1099-MISC	
			4 Federal income tax withheld $	Copy 1
PAYER'S federal identification number	RECIPIENT'S identification number	5 Fishing boat proceeds $	6 Medical and health care payments $	For State Tax Department
RECIPIENT'S name		7 Nonemployee compensation $	8 Substitute payments in lieu of dividends or interest $	
Street address (including apt. no.)		9 Payer made direct sales of $5,000 or more of consumer products to a buyer (recipient) for resale ▶ ☐	10 Crop insurance proceeds $	
City, state, and ZIP code		11	12	
Account number (see instructions)		13 Excess golden parachute payments $	14 Gross proceeds paid to an attorney $	
15a Section 409A deferrals $	15b Section 409A income $	16 State tax withheld $ $	17 State/Payer's state no.	18 State income $ $

Form 1099-MISC   Department of the Treasury - Internal Revenue Service

☐ CORRECTED (if checked)

PAYER'S name, street address, city, state, ZIP code, and telephone no.		1 Rents $	OMB No. 1545-0115	
		2 Royalties $	**2010** Form **1099-MISC**	**Miscellaneous Income**
		3 Other income $	4 Federal income tax withheld $	**Copy B** **For Recipient**
PAYER'S federal identification number	RECIPIENT'S identification number	5 Fishing boat proceeds $	6 Medical and health care payments $	
RECIPIENT'S name		7 Nonemployee compensation $	8 Substitute payments in lieu of dividends or interest $	This is important tax information and is being furnished to the Internal Revenue Service. If you are required to file a return, a negligence penalty or other sanction may be imposed on you if this income is taxable and the IRS determines that it has not been reported.
Street address (including apt. no.)		9 Payer made direct sales of $5,000 or more of consumer products to a buyer (recipient) for resale ► ☐	10 Crop insurance proceeds $	
City, state, and ZIP code		11	12	
Account number (see instructions)		13 Excess golden parachute payments $	14 Gross proceeds paid to an attorney $	
15a Section 409A deferrals $	15b Section 409A income $	16 State tax withheld $ $	17 State/Payer's state no.	18 State income $ $

Form **1099-MISC**   (keep for your records)   Department of the Treasury · Internal Revenue Service

Instructions for Recipient

Recipient's identification number. For your protection, this form may show only the last four digits of your social security number (SSN), individual taxpayer identification number (ITIN), or adoption taxpayer identification number (ATIN). However, the issuer has reported your complete identification number to the IRS and, where applicable, to state and/or local governments.

Account number. May show an account or other unique number the payer assigned to distinguish your account.

Amounts shown may be subject to self-employment (SE) tax. If your net income from self-employment is $400 or more, you must file a return and compute your SE tax on Schedule SE (Form 1040). See Pub. 334 for more information. If no income or social security and Medicare taxes were withheld and you are still receiving these payments, see Form 1040-ES. Individuals must report these amounts as explained in the box 7 instructions on this page. Corporations, fiduciaries, or partnerships must report the amounts on the proper line of their tax returns.

Form 1099-MISC incorrect? If this form is incorrect or has been issued in error, contact the payer. If you cannot get this form corrected, attach an explanation to your tax return and report your income correctly.

Boxes 1 and 2. Report rents from real estate on Schedule E (Form 1040). However, report rents on Schedule C or C-EZ (Form 1040) if you provided significant services to the tenant, sold real estate as a business, rented personal property as a business, or you and your spouse elected to be treated as a qualified joint venture. Report royalties from oil, gas, or mineral properties on Schedule E (Form 1040). However, report payments for a working interest as explained in the box 7 instructions. For royalties on timber, coal, and iron ore, see Pub. 544.

Box 3. Generally, report this amount on the "Other income" line of Form 1040 and identify the payment. The amount shown may be payments received as the beneficiary of a deceased employee, prizes, awards, taxable damages, Indian gaming profits, or other taxable income. See Pub. 525. If it is trade or business income, report this amount on Schedule C, C-EZ, or F (Form 1040).

Box 4. Shows backup withholding or withholding on Indian gaming profits. Generally, a payer must backup withhold at a 28% rate if you did not furnish your taxpayer identification number. See Form W-9 and Pub. 505 for more information. Report this amount on your income tax return as tax withheld.

Box 5. An amount in this box means the fishing boat operator considers you self-employed. Report this amount on Schedule C or C-EZ (Form 1040). See Pub. 334.

Box 6. For individuals, report on Schedule C or C-EZ (Form 1040).

Box 7. Shows nonemployee compensation. If you are in the trade or business of catching fish, box 7 may show cash you received for the sale of fish. If payments in this box are SE income, report this amount on Schedule C, C-EZ, or F (Form 1040), and complete Schedule SE (Form 1040). You received this form instead of Form W-2 because the payer did not consider you an employee and did not withhold income tax or social security and Medicare tax. If you believe you are an employee and cannot get the payer to correct this form, report the amount from box 7 on Form 1040, line 7 (or Form 1040NR, line 8). You must also complete Form 8919 and attach it to your return.

Box 8. Shows substitute payments in lieu of dividends or tax-exempt interest received by your broker on your behalf as a result of a loan of your securities. Report on the "Other income" line of Form 1040.

Box 9. If checked, $5,000 or more of sales of consumer products was paid to you on a buy-sell, deposit-commission, or other basis. A dollar amount does not have to be shown. Generally, report any income from your sale of these products on Schedule C or C-EZ (Form 1040).

Box 10. Report this amount on line 8 of Schedule F (Form 1040).

Box 13. Shows your total compensation of excess golden parachute payments subject to a 20% excise tax. See the Form 1040 instructions for where to report.

Box 14. Shows gross proceeds paid to an attorney in connection with legal services. Report only the taxable part as income on your return.

Box 15a. May show current year deferrals as a nonemployee under a nonqualified deferred compensation (NQDC) plan that is subject to the requirements of section 409A, plus any earnings on current and prior year deferrals.

Box 15b. Shows income as a nonemployee under an NQDC plan that does not meet the requirements of section 409A. This amount is also included in box 7 as nonemployee compensation. Any amount included in box 15a that is currently taxable is also included in this box. This income is also subject to a substantial additional tax to be reported on Form 1040. See "Total Tax" in the Form 1040 instructions.

Boxes 16-18. Shows state or local income tax withheld from the payments.

☐ CORRECTED (if checked)

PAYER'S name, street address, city, state, ZIP code, and telephone no.		1 Rents $	OMB No. 1545-0115	Miscellaneous Income
		2 Royalties $	2010 Form 1099-MISC	
		3 Other income $	4 Federal income tax withheld $	Copy 2
PAYER'S federal identification number	RECIPIENT'S identification number	5 Fishing boat proceeds $	6 Medical and health care payments $	To be filed with recipient's state income tax return, when required.
RECIPIENT'S name		7 Nonemployee compensation $	8 Substitute payments in lieu of dividends or interest $	
Street address (including apt. no.)		9 Payer made direct sales of $5,000 or more of consumer products to a buyer (recipient) for resale ▶ ☐	10 Crop insurance proceeds $	
City, state, and ZIP code		11	12	
Account number (see instructions)		13 Excess golden parachute payments $	14 Gross proceeds paid to an attorney $	
15a Section 409A deferrals $	15b Section 409A income $	16 State tax withheld $ $	17 State/Payer's state no.	18 State income $ $

Form **1099-MISC**

Department of the Treasury - Internal Revenue Service

☐ VOID ☐ CORRECTED		

PAYER'S name, street address, city, state, ZIP code, and telephone no.	**1** Rents $	OMB No. 1545-0115
	2 Royalties $	20**10** Form **1099-MISC**	Miscellaneous Income
	3 Other income $	**4** Federal income tax withheld $	Copy C For Payer
PAYER'S federal identification number	RECIPIENT'S identification number	**5** Fishing boat proceeds $	**6** Medical and health care payments $
RECIPIENT'S name	**7** Nonemployee compensation $	**8** Substitute payments in lieu of dividends or interest $	For Privacy Act and Paperwork Reduction Act Notice, see the **2010 General Instructions for Certain Information Returns.**
Street address (including apt. no.)	**9** Payer made direct sales of $5,000 or more of consumer products to a buyer (recipient) for resale ▶ ☐	**10** Crop insurance proceeds $	
City, state, and ZIP code	**11**	**12**	
Account number (see instructions)	2nd TIN not. ☐	**13** Excess golden parachute payments $	**14** Gross proceeds paid to an attorney $
15a Section 409A deferrals $	**15b** Section 409A income $	**16** State tax withheld $	**17** State/Payer's state no.	**18** State income $ $

Form **1099-MISC**   Department of the Treasury - Internal Revenue Service

Instructions for Payer

General and specific form instructions are provided as separate products. The products you should use to complete Form 1099-MISC are the 2010 General Instructions for Certain Information Returns and the 2010 Instructions for Form 1099-MISC. A chart in the general instructions gives a quick guide to which form must be filed to report a particular payment. To order these instructions and additional forms, visit the IRS website at *www.irs.gov* or call 1-800-TAX-FORM (1-800-829-3676).

Caution: *Because paper forms are scanned during processing, you cannot file with the IRS Forms 1096, 1098, 1099, 3921, 3922, or 5498 that you print from the IRS website.*

Due dates. Furnish Copy B of this form to the recipient by January 31, 2011. The due date is extended to February 15, 2011, if you are reporting payments in boxes 8 or 14.

File Copy A of this form with the IRS by February 28, 2011. If you file electronically, the due date is March 31, 2011. To file electronically, you must have software that generates a file according to the specifications in Pub. 1220, Specifications for Filing Forms 1098, 1099, 3921, 3922, 5498, 8935, and W-2G Electronically. IRS does not provide a fill-in form option.

Need help? If you have questions about reporting on Form 1099-MISC, call the information reporting customer service site toll free at 1-866-455-7438 or 304-263-8700 (not toll free). For TTY/TDD equipment, call 304-579-4827 (not toll free). The hours of operation are Monday through Friday 8:30 a.m. to 4:30 p.m., Eastern time.

Form 1099-DIV

Attention:

This form is provided for informational purposes only. Copy A appears in red, similar to the official IRS form. Do **not** file copy A downloaded from this website. The official printed version of this IRS form is scannable, but the online version of it, printed from this website, is not. A penalty of $50 per information return may be imposed for filing forms that cannot be scanned.

To order official IRS forms, call 1-800-TAX-FORM (1-800-829-3676) or Order Information Returns and Employer Returns Online, and we'll mail you the scannable forms and other products.

See IRS Publications 1141, 1167, 1179 and other IRS resources for information about printing these tax forms.

9191 ☐ VOID ☐ CORRECTED

PAYER'S name, street address, city, state, ZIP code, and telephone no.		1a Total ordinary dividends $	OMB No. 1545-0110	Dividends and Distributions
		1b Qualified dividends $	**2010** Form 1099-DIV	
		2a Total capital gain distr. $	2b Unrecap. Sec. 1250 gain $	Copy A For
PAYER'S federal identification number	RECIPIENT'S identification number	2c Section 1202 gain $	2d Collectibles (28%) gain $	Internal Revenue Service Center File with Form 1096.
RECIPIENT'S name		3 Nondividend distributions $	4 Federal income tax withheld $	For Privacy Act and Paperwork
			5 Investment expenses $	Reduction Act Notice, see the
Street address (including apt. no.)		6 Foreign tax paid $	7 Foreign country or U.S. possession	2010 General Instructions for Certain
City, state, and ZIP code		8 Cash liquidation distributions $	9 Noncash liquidation distributions $	Information Returns
Account number (see instructions)	2nd TIN not. ☐			

Form **1099-DIV**   Cat. No. 14415N   Department of the Treasury - Internal Revenue Service

Do Not Cut or Separate Forms on This Page — Do Not Cut or Separate Forms on This Page

☐ CORRECTED (if checked)

PAYER'S name, street address, city, state, ZIP code, and telephone no.		1a Total ordinary dividends $	OMB No. 1545-0110 20**10** Form **1099-DIV**	Dividends and Distributions
		1b Qualified dividends $		
		2a Total capital gain distr. $	2b Unrecap. Sec. 1250 gain $	Copy B
PAYER'S federal identification number	RECIPIENT'S identification number	2c Section 1202 gain $	2d Collectibles (28%) gain $	For Recipient
RECIPIENT'S name		3 Nondividend distributions $	4 **Federal income tax withheld** $	This is important tax information and is being furnished to the Internal Revenue Service. If you are required to file a return, a negligence penalty or other sanction may be imposed on you if this income is taxable and the IRS determines that it has not been reported.
			5 Investment expenses $	
Street address (including apt. no.)		6 Foreign tax paid $	7 Foreign country or U.S. possession	
City, state, and ZIP code		8 Cash liquidation distributions $	9 Noncash liquidation distributions $	
Account number (see instructions)				

Form **1099-DIV**   (keep for your records)   Department of the Treasury - Internal Revenue Service

Instructions for Recipient

Recipient's identification number. For your protection, this form may show only the last four digits of your social security number (SSN), individual taxpayer identification number (ITIN), or adoption taxpayer identification number (ATIN). However, the issuer has reported your complete identification number to the IRS and, where applicable, to state and/or local governments.

Account number. May show an account or other unique number the payer assigned to distinguish your account.

Box 1a. Shows total ordinary dividends that are taxable. Include this amount on line 9a of Form 1040 or 1040A. Also, report it on Schedule B (Form 1040) or Schedule 1 (Form 1040A), if required.

The amount shown may be dividends a corporation paid directly to you as a participant (or beneficiary of a participant) in an employee stock ownership plan (ESOP). Report it as a dividend on your Form 1040/1040A but treat it as a plan distribution, not as investment income, for any other purpose.

Box 1b. Shows the portion of the amount in box 1a that may be eligible for the 15% or zero capital gains rates. See the Form 1040/1040A instructions for how to determine this amount. Report the eligible amount on line 9b, Form 1040 or 1040A.

Box 2a. Shows total capital gain distributions from a regulated investment company or real estate investment trust. Report the amounts shown in box 2a on Schedule D (Form 1040), line 13. But, if no amount is shown in boxes 2c–2d and your only capital gains and losses are capital gain distributions, you may be able to report the amounts shown in box 2a on line 13 of Form 1040 (line 10 of Form 1040A) rather than Schedule D. See the Form 1040/1040A instructions.

Box 2b. Shows the portion of the amount in box 2a that is unrecaptured section 1250 gain from certain depreciable real property. Report this amount on the Unrecaptured Section 1250 Gain Worksheet–Line 19 in the Schedule D instructions (Form 1040).

Box 2c. Shows the portion of the amount in box 2a that is section 1202 gain from certain small business stock that may be subject to a 50% exclusion and certain empowerment zone business stock that may be subject to a 60% exclusion. See the Schedule D (Form 1040) instructions.

Box 2d. Shows 28% rate gain from sales or exchanges of collectibles. If required, use this amount when completing the 28% Rate Gain Worksheet–Line 18 in the instructions for Schedule D (Form 1040).

Box 3. Shows the part of the distribution that is nontaxable because it is a return of your cost (or other basis). You must reduce your cost (or other basis) by this amount for figuring gain or loss when you sell your stock. But if you get back all your cost (or other basis), report future distributions as capital gains. See Pub. 550, Investment Income and Expenses.

Box 4. Shows backup withholding. For example, a payer must backup withhold on certain payments at a 28% rate if you did not give your taxpayer identification number to the payer. See Form W-9, Request for Taxpayer Identification Number and Certification, for information on backup withholding. Include this amount on your income tax return as tax withheld.

Box 5. Shows your share of expenses of a nonpublicly offered regulated investment company, generally a nonpublicly offered mutual fund. If you file Form 1040, you may deduct these expenses on the "Other expenses" line on Schedule A (Form 1040) subject to the 2% limit. This amount is included in box 1a.

Box 6. Shows the foreign tax that you may be able to claim as a deduction or a credit on Form 1040. See the Form 1040 instructions.

Box 7. This box should be left blank if a regulated investment company reported the foreign tax shown in box 6.

Boxes 8 and 9. Shows cash and noncash liquidation distributions.

Nominees. If this form includes amounts belonging to another person, you are considered a nominee recipient. You must file Form 1099-DIV with the IRS for each of the other owners to show their share of the income, and you must furnish a Form 1099-DIV to each. A husband or wife is not required to file a nominee return to show amounts owned by the other. See the 2010 General Instructions for Certain Information Returns.

☐ VOID ☐ CORRECTED		
PAYER'S name, street address, city, state, ZIP code, and telephone no.	**1a** Total ordinary dividends $	OMB No. 1545-0110
	1b Qualified dividends $	2010 Dividends and Distributions
		Form **1099-DIV**
	2a Total capital gain distr. $	**2b** Unrecap. Sec. 1250 gain $	Copy C For Payer
PAYER'S federal identification number	RECIPIENT'S identification number	**2c** Section 1202 gain $	**2d** Collectibles (28%) gain $
RECIPIENT'S name	**3** Nondividend distributions $	**4** Federal income tax withheld $	For Privacy Act and Paperwork Reduction Act
		5 Investment expenses $	Notice, see the
Street address (including apt. no.)	**6** Foreign tax paid $	**7** Foreign country or U.S. possession	**2010 General Instructions for**
City, state, and ZIP code	**8** Cash liquidation distributions $	**9** Noncash liquidation distributions $	**Certain Information**
Account number (see instructions)	2nd TIN not. ☐		**Returns.**

Form **1099-DIV**   Department of the Treasury - Internal Revenue Service

Instructions for Payer

General and specific form instructions are provided as separate products. The products you should use to complete Form 1099-DIV are the 2010 General Instructions for Certain Information Returns and the 2010 Instructions for Form 1099-DIV. A chart in the general instructions gives a quick guide to which form must be filed to report a particular payment. To order these instructions and additional forms, visit the IRS website at *www.irs.gov* or call 1-800-TAX-FORM (1-800-829-3676).

Caution: *Because paper forms are scanned during processing, you cannot file with the IRS Forms 1096, 1098, 1099, 3921, 3922, or 5498 that you print from the IRS website.*

Due dates. Furnish Copy B of this form to the recipient by January 31, 2011.

File Copy A of this form with the IRS by February 28, 2011. If you file electronically, the due date is March 31, 2011. To file electronically, you must have software that generates a file according to the specifications in Pub. 1220, Specifications for Filing Forms 1098, 1099, 3921, 3922, 5498, 8935, and W-2G Electronically. IRS does not provide a fill-in form option.

Foreign dividend recipient. If the recipient of the dividend is a nonresident alien, you may have to withhold federal income tax and file Form 1042-S, Foreign Person's U.S. Source Income Subject to Withholding. See the Instructions for Form 1042-S and Pub. 515, Withholding of Tax on Nonresident Aliens and Foreign Entities.

Need help? If you have questions about reporting on Form 1099-DIV, call the information reporting customer service site toll free at 1-866-455-7438 or 304-263-8700 (not toll free). For TTY/TDD equipment, call 304-579-4827 (not toll free). The hours of operation are Monday through Friday from 8:30 a.m. to 4:30 p.m., Eastern time.

Examples of Complex Financial Statements

The first two statements are income statements.

Income Statement	
Sales	$2,000,000
Less: Cost of Goods Sold	1,100,00
Gross Profit	900,000
Less: Selling and Administrative Expense	200,000
Depreciation Expense	125,000
EBIT	575,000
Less: Interest Expense (10,800 + 33,000)	43,800
EBT	531,200
Less: Taxes (40%)	212,480
Net Earnings	$318, 720

A.E. Neuman Corporation
Income Statement For Year Ended December 31, 2010

Sales	$5,500,000
Less: Cost of Goods Sold	4,200,000
Gross Profit	1,300,000
Less: Selling and Administrative Expense	260,000
Operating Profit	1,040,000
Less: Depreciation Expense	150,000
Earnings Before Interest and Taxes	890,000
Less: Interest Expense	90,000
Earnings Before Taxes	800,000
Less: Taxes (50%)	400,000
Net Income	$400,000
Dividends Paid	$300,000

This next statement is an example of a more complex statement of cash flows.

Cash Flows from Operating Activities:		
Net Income (earnings after taxes)		$400,000
Adjustments:		
Add Back Depreciation	150,000	
Decrease in Marketable Securities	15,000	
Decrease in Accounts Receivable	20,000	
Increase in Inventories	(45,000)	
Decrease in Accounts Payable	(25,000)	
Decrease in Notes Payable	(55,000)	
Decrease in Accrued Expenses	(25,000)	
Increase in Incomes Taxes Payable	5,000	
Total Adjustments		40,000
Net Cash Flows from Operating Activities		$440,000
Cash Flows from Investing Activities		
Decrease in Investments	15,000	
Increase in Plant & Equipment	(250,000)	
Net Cash Flows from Investing Activities		(235,000)
Cash Flows from Financing Activities		
Increase in Bonds Payable	100,000	
Dividends Paid	(300,000)	
Net Cash Flows from Financing Activities		(200,000)
Net Increase (Decrease) in Cash Flows		5,000

Endnotes

Preface

[1] Keith H. Hammonds, "Why We Hate HR," *Fast Company*, August 1, 2005. Available at www.fastcompany.com/magazine/97/open_hr.html.

Chapter 1

[1] Mason A. Carpenter and Wm. Gerard Sanders, *Strategic Management* (New Jersey: Pearson Prentice Hall, 2009).

[2] Ibid.

[3] Linda Martin and David G. Mutchler, *Fail-Safe Leadership: Straight Talk About Correcting the Leadership Challenges in Your Organization* (New York: Delta Books, 2003).

Chapter 2

[1] Dave Ulrich et al, *HR Competencies: Mastery at the Intersection of People and Business* (Alexandria, VA: Society for Human Resource Management, 2008).

[2] Sarbanes-Oxley Act of 2002 (Pub.L. 107-204, 116 Stat. 745). Available at www.gpo.gov/fdsys/pkg/PLAW-107publ204/pdf/PLAW -107publ204.pdf.

[3] Barbara Kiviat, "Q&A: Starbucks Can Smell Growth," *TIME*, February 1, 2010. Available at www.time.com/time/magazine /article/0,9171,1955588,00.html#ixzz1Ebf7HaOn.

Chapter 3

[1] John J. Wild, Leopold A. Bernstein, and K.R. Subramanyam, *Financial Statement Analysis*, 7th edition (New York: McGraw Hill, 2000), p. 21.

Chapter 4

[1] Joseph L. Badaracco Jr., *Leading Quietly: An Unorthodox Guide to Doing the Right Thing* (Boston, Harvard Business School Press, 2002).

[2] Stanley Block, Geoffrey Hirt, and Bartley Danielsen, *Foundations of Financial Management*, 13th edition (New York: McGraw Hill, 2009).

Chapter 7

[1] Block, Hirt, and Danielsen (2009).

[2] Wild, Bernstein, and Subramanyam (2000).

Chapter 8

[1] Block, Hirt, and Danielsen (2009).

Chapter 9

[1] See "Return On Equity—ROE," Investopedia. Available at www.investopedia.com/terms/r/returnonequity.asp.

[2] See "ROE," Russell Investments, available at www.russell.com/us/glossary/accounting/roe.htm.

[3] An interesting analysis of the nature of risk and people management is Andrew Lambert and David Cooper, "Managing the People Dimension of Risk," *CRF Research*, August 2010. This report takes a more global and qualitative perspective on the question of risk management and human resources.

[4] Annual Statement Studies: Financial Ratio Benchmarks. Risk Management Association, Publisher. Philadelphia, PA, 2010.

Chapter 10

[1] See, for example, Howard Schilit and Jeremy Perler, *Financial Shenanigans: How to Detect Accounting Gimmicks & Fraud in Financial Reports*, 3d edition (New York: McGraw-Hill, 2010); Paul M. Clikeman, *Called to Account: Fourteen Financial Frauds that Shaped the American Accounting Profession* (New York: Routledge, 2008); and Ken Fisher and Lara W. Hoffmans, *How to Smell a Rat: The Five Signs of Financial Fraud* (Hoboken, NJ: Wiley, 2010).

[2] Garey, Regan (2008) *Ethical Standards: Legislate or Rely on a Principles-Based Accounting System.*

[3] Garey, Regan (2007) *The Role of Emotionally Intelligent Leaders in Supplanting the Need for the Sarbanes-Oxley Act Whistleblower Provision.*

[4] Garey, Regan (2008).

[5] "Basic Control Activities," Audit and Management Advisory Services, Syracuse University. See http://amas.syr.edu/AMAS/display.cfm?content_ID=%23%28%28%25%2B%0A.

[6] Garey, Regan (2007).

[7] Elizabeth D. Hart, James M. McGrath, and Mitchel E. Sekler, "HR and Accounting: What the HR Professional Needs to Know," *Human Resources*, Winter 2007, 65-71. Available at www.cadwalader.com/assets/article/110106WhatHRProfessionalNeedstoKnow.pdf.

[8] Garey, Regan (2008).

[9] Ibid.

[10] Ibid.

[11] Ibid.

[12] Jerry L. Turner, Theodore J. Mock, and Rajendra P. Srivastava, "An Analysis of the Fraud Triangle," January 2003. Available at http://aaahq.org/audit/midyear/03midyear/papers/Research%20Roundtable%203-Turner-Mock-Srivastava.pdf.

[13] Garey, Regan (2008).

[14] J. Harrison, "Where Does the Target Stand on Fraud Prevention?" *Mergers & Acquisitions: The Dealermaker's Journal* (2004).

[15] Ibid.

[16] Lewis Dulitz, "IFRS: A Preparer's Point of View," *Journal of Accountancy*, April 2009, 46-49. Available at www.journalofaccountancy. com/Issues/2009/Apr/PreparersPointofView.htm.

Index

About the Author

Dr. Regan W. Garey is a full-time member of the Business Department faculty at Immaculata University in Southeastern Pennsylvania. Her areas of teaching include financial accounting, finance, and tax.

She is a CPA and has experience as an accountant and business owner. Her consulting business focuses on training individuals on a wide variety of business topics. Her independent consulting (www.acctliteracy.com) led her to writing this book. Dr. Garey often speaks to SHRM groups about various topics, including emotional intelligence and business literacy.

She is an active member of the community and she enjoys working with the Food Bank of Delaware as a member of the Board of Trustees.

She and her husband enjoy travel and outdoor activities, especially skiing. They have two grown children.

Contact Dr. Garey with any questions related to this book or financial literacy: regangarey@yahoo.com

Additional SHRM-Published Books

101 Sample Write-Ups for Documenting Employee Performance Problems: A Guide to Progressive Discipline & Termination
By Paul Falcone

Assessing External Job Candidates
By Jean M. Phillips and Stanley M. Gully

Assessing Internal Job Candidates
By Jean M. Phillips and Stanley M. Gully

Becoming the Evidence-Based Manager: Making the Science of Management Work for You
By Gary P. Latham

The Cultural Fit Factor: Creating an Employment Brand That Attracts, Retains, and Repels the Right Employees
By Lizz Pellet

Employment Termination Source Book
By Wendy Bliss and Gene Thornton

The Essential Guide to Federal Employment Laws
By Lisa Guerin and Amy DelPo

The Essential Guide to Workplace Investigations: How to Handle Employee Complaints & Problems
By Lisa Guerin

From Hello to Goodbye: Proactive Tips for Maintaining Positive Employee Relations
By Christine V. Walters

Got a Minute? The 9 Lessons Every HR Professional Must Learn to Be Successful
By Dale J. Dwyer and Sheri A. Caldwell

HR Competencies: Mastery at the Intersection of People and Business
By Dave Ulrich, Wayne Brockbank, Dani Johnson, Kurt Sandholtz, and Jon Younger

Human Resource Essentials: Your Guide to Starting and Running the HR Function
By Lin Grensing-Pophal

Investing in What Matters: Linking Employees to Business Outcomes
By Scott P. Mondore and Shane S. Douthitt

Leading with Your Heart: Diversity and *Ganas* for Inspired Inclusion
By Cari M. Dominguez and Jude Sotherlund

The Legal Context of Staffing
By Jean M. Phillips and Stanley M. Gully

The Manager's Guide to HR: Hiring, Firing, Performance Evaluations, Documentation, Benefits, and Everything Else You Need to Know
By Max Muller

Never Get Lost Again: Navigating Your HR Career
By Nancy E. Glube and Phyllis G. Hartman

Performance Appraisal Source Book
By Mike Deblieux

Proving the Value of HR: How and Why to Measure ROI
By Jack J. Phillips and Patricia Pulliam Phillips

Rethinking Retention in Good Times and Bad: Breakthrough Ideas for Keeping Your Best Workers
By Richard P. Finnegan

Staffing Forecasting and Planning
By Jean M. Phillips and Stanley M. Gully

Staffing to Support Business Strategy
By Jean M. Phillips and Stanley M. Gully

Stop Bullying at Work: Strategies and Tools for HR and Legal Professionals
By Teresa A. Daniel